OECD Reviews on Local Job Creation

Employment and Skills Strategies in Israel

This work is published under the responsibility of the Secretary-General of the OECD. The opinions expressed and arguments employed herein do not necessarily reflect the official views of OECD member countries.

This document and any map included herein are without prejudice to the status of or sovereignty over any territory, to the delimitation of international frontiers and boundaries and to the name of any territory, city or area.

Please cite this publication as:
OECD (2015), *Employment and Skills Strategies in Israel*, OECD Reviews on Local Job Creation, OECD Publishing, Paris.
http://dx.doi.org/10.1787/9789264232969-en

ISBN 978-92-64-23295-2 (print)
ISBN 978-92-64-23296-9 (PDF)

Serie: OECD Reviews on Local Job Creation
ISSN 2311-2328 (print)
ISSN 2311-2336 (online)

The statistical data for Israel are supplied by and under the responsibility of the relevant Israeli authorities. The use of such data by the OECD is without prejudice to the status of the Golan Heights, East Jerusalem and Israeli settlements in the West Bank under the terms of international law.

Photo credits: Cover © Andy Dean Photography/Shutterstock.com, © Pakhnyushchy/Shutterstock.com

Corrigenda to OECD publications may be found on line at: *www.oecd.org/about/publishing/corrigenda.htm*.

© OECD 2015

You can copy, download or print OECD content for your own use, and you can include excerpts from OECD publications, databases and multimedia products in your own documents, presentations, blogs, websites and teaching materials, provided that suitable acknowledgement of OECD as source and copyright owner is given. All requests for public or commercial use and translation rights should be submitted to *rights@oecd.org*. Requests for permission to photocopy portions of this material for public or commercial use shall be addressed directly to the Copyright Clearance Center (CCC) at *info@copyright.com* or the Centre français d'exploitation du droit de copie (CFC) at *contact@cfcopies.com*.

Preface

Across the OECD, policy-makers are grappling with a critical question: how to create jobs? The recent financial crisis and economic downturn has had serious consequences across most OECD countries, with rising unemployment rates and jobs being lost across many sectors. Indeed, for some countries, the effects the downturn brought with it are continuing, if not amplifying. Shrinking public budgets in some countries also mean that policy makers must now do more with less. In this context, it is necessary to think laterally about how actions in one area, such as employment and training, can have simultaneous benefits in others, such as creating new jobs and better supporting labour market inclusion.

Over recent years, the work of the OECD LEED Programme on Designing Local Skills Strategies, *Building Flexibility and Accountability into Local Employment Services, Breaking out of Policy Silos, Leveraging Training and Skills Development in SMEs*, and *Skills for Competitiveness* has demonstrated that local strategies to boost skills and job creation require the participation of many different actors across employment, training, economic development, and social welfare portfolios. Employers, unions and the non-profit sector are also key partners in ensuring that education and training programmes provide the skills needed in the labour markets of today and the future.

The *OECD Reviews on Local Job Creation* deliver evidence-based and practical recommendations on how to better support employment and economic development at the local level. This report builds on sub-national data analysis and consultations at the national level and with local stakeholders in two case study areas. It provides a comparative framework to understand the role of the local level in contributing to more and better quality jobs. The report can help national and local policy makers in Israel build effective and sustainable partnerships, which join-up efforts and achieve stronger outcomes across employment, training, and economic development policies. Co-ordinated policies can help workers find suitable jobs, while also stimulating entrepreneurship and productivity, which increases the quality of life and prosperity within a community as well as throughout the country.

I would like to warmly thank the Prime Minister's Office and the Ministry of Industry, Trade and Labour of Israel for their active participation and support of the study.

Sergio Arzeni,
Director, OECD Centre for Entrepreneurship,
SMEs and Local Development

Acknowledgments

This review has been written by the Local Economic and Employment Development (LEED) Programme of the Organisation for Economic Co-operation and Development (OECD) as part of a project undertaken in co-operation with the Prime Minister's Office and the Ministry of Industry, Trade and Labour of Israel. This project is part of the OECD LEED programme of work under the leadership of Sylvain Giguère.

The principal authors are Daniel Felsenstein (Hebrew University of Jerusalem) and Jonathan Barr, Policy Analyst, OECD. The authors would like to thank Francesca Froy, Senior Policy Analyst, OECD for her comments on the report. Thanks also go to Michela Meghnagi for her work on the data analysis, as well as Elisa Campestrin, François Iglesias, Malika Taberkane and other colleagues in the OECD LEED Programme for their assistance with the preparation of this report.

The authors would also like to acknowledge the valuable contributions of Dan Feldman and Asrar Kayal who served as research assistants for the duration of this project and Chris Warhurst (Director at the Institute for Employment Research University of Warwick) for his contributions to this report and participation on the project study visit.

Finally, special thanks are given to the national and local representatives who participated in the project interviews and roundtables, and provided documentation and comments critical to the production of the report.

Table of contents

Acronyms and abbreviations 10
Executive summary 11
Key recommendations 12
Reader's guide 14
Local job creation dashboard 10
The approach for Israel 11
Chapter 1. Policy context for employment and skills in Israel 17
Economic and labour market trends 18
Regional economic growth 19
Active labour market policy instruments 21
Mapping the institutional framework for employment and skills 23
Constraints to increased labour market participation of the Arab-Israeli Minority 26
References 28
Chapter 2. Overview of the Israel case study areas 29
Overview of the case study regions 30
Labour force trends across the case study areas 31
Regression analysis of wages and participation rate 35
Balance between skills supply and demand at the sub-national level 36
Conclusions 39
References 40
Chapter 3. Local job creation dashboard findings in Israel 41
Theme 1: Better aligning policy and programmes to local economic development 42
Theme 2: Adding value through skills 47
Theme 3: Targeting policy to local employment sectors and investing in quality jobs 51
Theme 4: Being inclusive 54
References 58
Chapter 4. Towards an action plan for jobs in Israel: Recommendations and best practices 61
Better aligning programmes and policies to local economic development 62
Adding value through skills 66
Targeting policy to local employment sectors and investing in quality jobs 70
Being inclusive 74
References 75
Annex A. Communities included in the study area 77
Annex B. Gross regional product estimates 78
Annex C. Comparing labour market outcomes in the case study areas 79
Annex D. Regression results 87

Tables

Table 1.1 Government expenditures on active labour market policies, 2008-2011 22
Table 2.1 Key economic and labour maket outcomes across the case study areas, 2011 32
Table D.1 Panel regressions for wages and labour participation rate (t stats in parentheses) 87

Figures

Figure 1.1 Unemployment rate before and after the crisis, OECD countries 18
Figure 1.2 Gross regional product as percentage of national GDP, Israel, 2000-2010 21
Figure 1.3 Expenditure for ALMP as % of GDP, 2011 22
Figure 1.4 Institutional framework for employment, skills, and economic development policies 25
Figure 2.1 Overview of case study areas... 30
Figure 2.2 Understanding the relationship between skills supply and demand.................. 37
Figure 2.3 Balancing skills supply and demand in Israel, 2005 38
Figure 2.4 Balancing skills supply and demand in Israel, 2010 38
Figure 3.1 Local job creation dashboard results for Israel 42
Figure 3.2 Dashboard results for better aligning policy and programmes to local economic development 43
Figure 3.3 Capacity of local public employment service offices to deliver their objectives......... 44
Figure 3.4 Which organisations does the public employment service collaborate with at the local level? 45
Figure 3.5 Dashboard results for adding value through skills.............................. 47
Figure 3.6 Types of activities that are delivered, funded, or referred by the public employment service to people from minorities.. 49
Figure 3.7 Dashboard results for targeting policy to local employment sectors and investing in quality jobs 51
Figure 3.8 Dashboard results for being inclusive 54
Figure 3.9 Types of work undertaken by the public employment service with employers regarding minority groups 55
Figure C.1 Male wages, 2000-20111 79
Figure C.2 Female wages, 2000-2011 79
Figure C.3 Female labour market participation by sub-district, 2000-2011 80
Figure C.4 Male labour force participation by sub-district, 2000-2011......................... 80
Figure C.5 Youth labour force participation by sub-district, 2000-2010........................ 81
Figure C.6 Labour force participation of older works (over 50 years), 2000-2010................ 81
Figure C.7 Female unemployment by sub-district, 2000-2011 82
Figure C.8 Male unemployment by sub-district, 2000-2010................................. 82
Figure C.9 Youth unemployment (15-24) by sub-district, 2000-2010.......................... 83
Figure C.10 Unemployment among older workers (over 50 years), 2000-2010 83
Figure C.11 Job search: proportion actively looking for work- Jewish and Arab female labour force, 2000-2011 84
Figure C.12 Job search: proportion actively looking for work - Jewish and Arab male labour force, 2000-2011 84
Figure C.13 Arab female labour force, 1-8 yrs and 16+ yrs education, 2000-2011................. 85
Figure C.14 Arab male labour force, 1-8 yrs and 16+ yrs education, 2000-2011 86

Boxes

Box 1 Summary of the OECD LEED Local Job Creation Project Methodology. 14
Box 2 Local Job Creation Dashboard. 15
Box 1.1 Employment Orientation Centres: providing one-stop services for the Arab-Israeli population. 21
Box 2.2 Explaining the diagnostic tool 37
Box 3.1 INJAZ Centre for the professionalization of Arab local government 46
Box 3.2 Targeting training to the long-term unemployed and Arab-Israelis. 49
Box 3.3 Nazareth Small Business Development Centre (MATI) 53
Box 3.4 The Al Bawader investment fund. 54
Box 3.5 The Abraham Fund. 56
Box 4.1 How to build successful partnerships?. 63
Box 4.2 The What Works Centre in the United Kingdom. 65
Box 4.3 Recent apprenticeship initiatives within the United States 67
Box 4.4 OECD experiences in providing career guidance 69
Box 4.5 Practice labs for innovative work organisation, Flanders, Belgium. 72
Box 4.6 Entrepreneurship programmes for youth 73
Box 4.7 Using public procurement for social inclusion, city of Most, Czech Republic 74

Acronyms and abbreviations

AEDA	Authority for the Economic Development of the Arab Sector
ALMP	Active Labour Market Policy
BOI	Bank of Israel
CBS	Central Bureau of Statistics
EITC	Earned Income Tax Credit
EOC	Employment Orientation Center
GRP	Gross Regional Product
HE	Higher Education
JDC-TEVET	Joint Distribution Committee (Humanitarian NGO) TEVET: poverty to employment program
LA	Local Authority
LECI	Law for the Encouragement of Capital Investment
MDGN	Ministry for the Development of the Galilee and the Negev
MED	Ministry of Education
MIA	Ministry of Immigrant Absorption
MOE	Ministry of Economy
MOF	Ministry of Finance
MOITAL	Minsitry of Industry Trade and Labor (now called MOE)
MOW	Ministry of Welfare
MTDB	Manpower Training and Development Bureau
NGO	Non Governmental Organization
OCS	Office of the Chief Scientist (at the MOE)
OJT	On the Job Training
PS	Private Sector
PES	Public Employment Service
SBA	SmallBusiness Authority
SBDC	Small Business Development Center
VET	Vocational and Educational Training

Executive summary

While Israel weathered the global financial crisis relatively well compared to other OECD countries and unemployment remains at historically low levels, there are a number of disadvantaged groups, who face significant labour market challenges, including Arab-Israelis and the Ultra-Orthodox (Haredim). This report focuses on the specific challenges facing the Arab-Israeli population and government policies which have been introduced to increase their labour market participation.

The OECD Local Economic and Employment Development (LEED) Programme has developed the *Local Job Creation* reviews as an international cross-comparative study examining the contribution of local labour market policy to boosting quality employment and productivity. In Israel, the review has looked at the range of institutions and bodies involved in employment and skills policies. In-depth work was undertaken in two case study areas which include the Haifa and Yizreel sub-districts.

Employment Orientation Centres have been introduced by the government, designed as one-stop shops providing culturally sensitive services to the Arab population. These centres are a welcome development to target the Arab-Israeli population but it is important that their work is well integrated with current training and economic development activities at the local level. To be successful, these centres will need to be well coordinated with services such as public transportation and child care, which remain important barriers for many Arab-Israelis to effectively participate in the labour market. These centres can serve as anchor organisations within their community, stimulating partnerships with other organisations in serving the Arab-Israeli population.

The results of this study indicate the adverse impacts of potential skills mismatches as they relate to the effect of working outside the locality of residence. This study finds that working locally has a positive and significant effect on labour force participation. Increasing non-commuting (e.g. working locally) by 1% leads to 5% growth in Arab labour market participation and 3% growth in female Arab labour market participation.

Skills are a key route out of poverty but many disadvantaged groups in Israel have levels of skills attainment well below that of the mainstream Jewish population. It is important that the government focuses on expanding the quality and accessibility of the vocational education and training system. This will give Arab-Israelis good access to skills development opportunities that are well connected to the world of work. In particular, the government should examine how to increase the quality of the apprenticeship and work-based training system. Targeted programmes could be designed for Arab-Israelis to provide them with relevant on the job training opportunities and equip them for labour market success.

A key feature of employment services, including the Employment Orientation Centres within Israel is placing people into jobs. While this is important, it is also critical to ensure that job placements provide quality and sustainable employment opportunities. Individuals with insufficient skills will not be able to retain a job over the long-term therefore more attention needs to be given to basic skills training opportunities within employment services.

Employers will be critical partners in ensuring that the employment and training system is well connected to the needs of the labour market. They should be better connected and engaged in the design and delivery of skills development programmes. It will also be important to ensure that the secondary education system is well linked to employment and training services so that youth have good information upon which to make labour market decisions. This requires a comprehensive career guidance system to be developed which focuses on local job opportunities and the required qualifications.

There are opportunities to stimulate overall job quality and productivity by working with employers on the better utilisation of skills. This would mean focusing on how to design jobs in a way, which takes account of an individual's potential and provides career progression and mobility opportunities into better jobs with higher wages.

Lastly, there is also an opportunity to strategically use public procurement to build quality employment at the local level. Tenders could contain specific provisions, which are geared towards increasing participation of the Arab-Israeli population.

Key recommendations

Better aligning programmes and policies to local economic development

- Strengthen local policy cooperation and coordination by fostering partnerships, which can effectively design and implement employment and skills strategies targeted at Arab-Israelis.
- Build effective monitoring and evaluation systems at the local level to understand what works in effectively removing labour market barriers and stimulating job creation and economic development opportunities.

Adding value through skills

- Increase the overall level of skills of the Arab-Israeli population through stronger skills development opportunities.
- Create more apprenticeship and on the job training opportunities for Arab-Israelis.
- Introduce effective career guidance systems targeted to Arab-Israelis, which ease school to work transitions and create transparent pathways which better connect high schools to the world of work.

Targeting policy to local employment sectors and investing in quality jobs

- Place a stronger emphasis on the quality of jobs and the better utilisation of skills to stimulate overall productivity within the local labour market.
- Continue to stimulate entrepreneurship opportunities among the Arab-Israeli population to create more and better jobs.

Being inclusive

- Use government procurement more strategically by establishing conditions within contracts to support inclusive growth and increase labour force participation among Arab-Israelis.

Reader's guide

The *Local Job Creation* project involves a series of country reviews in Australia, Belgium (Flanders), Canada (Ontario and Quebec), Czech Republic, France, Ireland, Israel, Italy (Autonomous Province of Trento), Korea, Sweden, the United Kingdom and the United States (California and Michigan). The key stages of each review are summarised in Box 1.

Box 1. **Summary of the OECD LEED Local Job Creation Project Methodology**

- Analyse available data to understand the key labour market challenges facing the country in the context of the economic recovery and apply an OECD LEED diagnostic tool which seeks to assess the balance between the supply and demand for skills at the local level
- Map the current policy framework for local job creation in the country
- Apply the local job creation dashboard, developed by the OECD LEED Programme (Froy et al, 2010) to measure the relative strengths and weaknesses of local employment and training agencies to contribute to job creation
- Distribute an electronic questionnaire to local employment offices to gather information on how they work with other stakeholders to support local job creation policies
- Conduct an OECD study visit, where local and national roundtables with a diverse range of stakeholders are held to discuss the results and refine the findings and recommendations
- Contribute to policy development in the reviewed country by proposing policy options to overcome barriers, illustrated by selected good practice initiatives from other OECD countries

While the economic crisis is the current focus of policy-makers, there is a need for both short-term and longer-term actions to ensure sustainable economic growth. In response to this issue, the OECD LEED Programme has developed a set of thematic areas on which local stakeholders and employment and training agencies can focus to build sustainable growth at the local level. These include:

1. **Better aligning policies and programmes to local economic development challenges and opportunities;**
2. **Adding value through skills:** Creating an adaptable skilled labour force and supporting employment progression and skills upgrading;
3. **Targeting policy to local employment sectors and investing in quality jobs**, including gearing education and training to emerging local growth sectors and responding to global trends, while working with employers on skills utilisation and productivity; and,

4. **Being inclusive** to ensure that all actual and potential members of the labour force can contribute to future economic growth.

Local job creation dashboard

As part of the project, the LEED Programme has drawn on its previous research to develop a set of best practice priorities in each thematic area, which is used to assess local practice through the local job creation dashboard (see Box 2). The dashboard enables national and local policy-makers to gain a stronger overview of the strengths and weaknesses of the current policy framework, whilst better prioritising future actions and resources. A value between 1 (low) to 5 (high) is assigned to each of the four priority areas corresponding to the relative strengths and weaknesses of local policy approaches based on best practices in other OECD countries.

Box 2. Local Job Creation Dashboard

Better aligning policies and programmes to local economic development

1.1. Flexibility in the delivery of employment and vocational training policies
1.2. Capacities within employment and VET sectors
1.3. Policy co-ordination, policy integration and co-operation with other sectors
1.4. Evidence based policy making

Adding value through skills

2.1. Flexible training open to all in a broad range of sectors
2.2. Working with employers on training
2.3. Matching people to jobs and facilitating progression
2.4. Joined up approaches to skills

Targeting policy to local employment sectors and investing in quality jobs

3.1. Relevance of provision to important local employment sectors and global trends and challenges
3.2. Working with employers on skills utilisation and productivity
3.3. Promotion of skills for entrepreneurship
3.4. Promoting quality jobs through local economic development

Being inclusive

4.1. Employment and training programmes geared to local "at-risk" groups
4.2. Childcare and family friendly policies to support women's participation in employment
4.3. Tackling youth unemployment
4.4. Openness to immigration

The approach for Israel

This study has looked at the range of institutions and bodies involved in workforce and skills development in Israel. On joining the OECD in 2010, Israel committed to a series of labour market and social policy reforms, foremost of which was the enhancement of employment opportunities for disadvantaged populations. This report focuses on employment and skills strategies targeting the integration of the Arab-Israeli population. In-depth analysis was undertaken to look at local employment and economic development activities in two contiguous yet distinct, geographic regions:

- the Haifa sub-district; and
- the Yizreel sub-district.

In each case study area, interviews were conducted with a wide set of stakeholders. An electronic questionnaire was also sent to local managers within public employment service offices across Israel, requesting information on their local job creation activities. The questionnaire was administrated during the first quarter of 2014 and the results are based on 25 valid responses. The Northern district gave 40% of the responses, followed by Jerusalem (24%) and the Central district (12%).

In March 2014, two local roundtables were held in each of the case study areas and at the national level to discuss the findings and recommendations. These meetings brought together a range of stakeholders, including relevant department officials in the fields of employment, economic development, and training; employers; and other local community and social development organisations.

References

Froy, F., S. Giguère and E. Travkina (2010), *Local Job Creation: Project Methodology*, OECD Local Economic and Employment Development (LEED), OECD, Paris, www.oecd.org/cfe/leed/Local%20Job%20Creation%20Methodology_27%20February.pdf.

Chapter 1

Policy context for employment and skills in Israel*

This chapter provides an overview of Israel's employment and skills system. While Israel has weathered the global financial crisis better than most OECD countries and unemployment remains at historically low levels, there are wide differences in labour market outcomes across certain population groups. Arab-Israelis and Ultra-orthodox (Haredim) face a number of unique labour market challenges and have labour force participation rates significantly below that of the mainstream Jewish population.

* The statistical data for Israel are supplied by and under the responsibility of the relevant Israeli authorities. The use of such data by the OECD is without prejudice to the status of the Golan Heights, East Jerusalem and Israeli settlements in the West Bank under the terms of international law.

Economic and labour market trends

Over the last decade, Israel has experienced a period of strong economic growth and unemployment has remained relatively low. The global economic crisis had severe labour market repercussions in many advanced countries but less of an impact on the Israeli economy. Over this period, Israel's unemployment rate averaged 6.5% compared to the OECD average unemployment rate of 8.2% between 2008-2013 (see Figure 1.1). The OECD's recent *Economic Survey of Israel* notes that output growth has been impressive, considering global economic weakness and the unemployment rate is at a 30 year low (OECD, 2013a).

Figure 1.1 **Unemployment rate before and after the crisis, OECD countries**

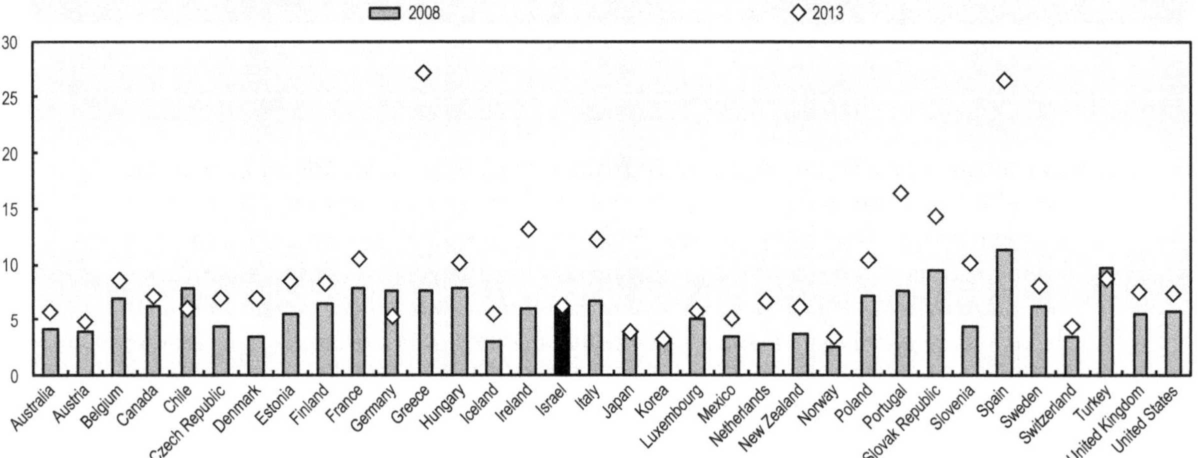

Source: OECD (2013), "Unemployment rate", *Employment and Labour Markets: Key Tables from OECD*, No. 1. doi: http://dx.doi.org/10.1787/unemp-table-2013-1-en

Uniquely in Israel, the share of the lower income groups in overall income has grown relative to those at the top (Ben David, 2012). This has probably occurred because of the growth in participation rates among low income individuals and the increased number of earners per household. While gaps in income per capita and labour productivity relative to the top half of the OECD have been narrowing since 2002-03, they remain substantial (OECD, 2013a). The latest OECD Economic Survey of Israel points out that while there has been a welcome increase in employment among vulnerable groups, this has yet to translate into sustained reductions in poverty, underscoring a problem of in-work poverty, especially among households with one income earners (OECD, 2013a).

Improving living standards is particularly important for the Arab-Israeli and Ultra-orthodox (Haredim) populations, whose labour market outcomes are significantly below the mainstream Jewish population. In 2012, the overall labour force participation rate of Israel was 66% compared to an OECD average of 77% (OECD, 2012b). However, the labour force participation rate is significantly lower for Arab-Israelis (52%) and ultra-orthodox (Haredim) Jews (45%). Both groups also have high shares of poverty with at least half of the Arab population and 60% of the Haredi population under the poverty line (OECD, 2010).

Within Israel's mainly urban population, about 75% are Jewish and most of the remaining 25% are Arab-Israelis (about 20% of the total population). In the 1990s, a wave of relatively well-educated Jewish immigrants from Russia, (now accounting for 8% of the population) filled the need for higher level technical and engineering skills within the economy but many of these migrants are now approaching retirement (OECD, 2013a; OECD, 2013b). This will have a strong impact on the skills needs of the labour market in the future.

A high level of education is common in Israel with 46% of adults (e.g. 25-64 years old) having a tertiary degree in 2012 compared with 33% on average for OECD countries (OECD, 2014). A high level of skills also translates into positive labour market outcomes in Israel as the employment rates for adults (25-64 year-olds) with a tertiary education was 85% compared with 47% among those without an upper secondary education.

Internationally, the trend towards higher level skills has increased the return to higher education and increased inequality in some OECD countries. Public policy in Israel has tried to encourage weaker sub groups to increase their labour force participation and widen the earnings base. The result has been a sizeable increase in employment rates especially among women, and particularly amongst those sub populations identified with low employment rates and high poverty levels such as Arab women, ultra-Orthodox Jewish women and those with low or no education levels.

The increase in female participation has increased the population of two-earner households in Israel but has impacted on the phenomenon of the 'working poor'. In fact, male participation amongst those with little schooling has not increased and has stagnated. These trends differ from those in most OECD countries where male and female labour market patterns and earnings tend to become more similar over time.

Low participation amongst Israeli-Arabs relates to the participation of low educated mothers with large families as well as the early retirement of Arab males. These two sub- groups display unusual participation patterns over the life cycle. Arab women are characterized by very low levels of participation (28%). For Arab males, participation rises to levels commensurate with the general population but falls sharply after the age of 45. The drop off rate is more severe than in Europe (where it occurs in the 50-54 cohort) and in the United States (where it declines in the 55-59 group) (Yashiv and Kasir, 2011). It is even more severe than in other Arab and Muslim countries such as Jordan or Turkey. This phenomenon is probably related to the high prevalence of employment in manual labour occupations among Arab-Israeli males with the steep decline of physical capability with age.

For Arab women, the participation rate is low in comparison to Western countries and to Jewish women but is not significantly lower than that of women in other Arab and Muslim countries (Yashiv and Kasir 2013a). However a distinctive characteristic of Israeli-Arab female participation is its large variance. This is explained by various socio-demographic factors such as education, number of children and skills levels. Taken together, education and training can be seen as a key route to raising overall labour force participation.

Regional economic growth

National GDP growth in Israel has been around 3-4% in recent years, down from 5% in the mid-2000s. While Israel has weathered the worldwide economic downturn better than many OECD countries, the decrease in global demand has affected Israel primarily through reduced exports, which affects domestic consumption. The growth of the economy's productive capacity has bolstered resilience and has allowed labour supply to grow through increasing labour force participation rates. The growth in the participation rate has lowered labour productivity, which stands at 25% lower than the OECD average (OECD, 2013).

At the regional level, it is hard to identify these macro trends as unlike other advanced economies, Israel does not publish gross regional product (GRP) or regional GDP data (OECD, 2011). The spatial distribution of productive capacity provides the infrastructure upon which labour market change takes place. Therefore it is necessary to have an overview the distribution of GRP in order to anticipate demand for labour. In the absence of official data, this report uses a top-down allocation method for generating GRP estimates. This method proportionally allocates GRP to the regions on the basis of return to regional capital, workers compensation and housing services. This contrasts to the alternative (regional input-output) approach that generates individual accounts for each region. The estimation method and data sources are elaborated in Annex B.

The data in Figure 1.2 shows the metropolitan dominance of Tel Aviv and the Central Districts. This level of economic concentration puts Tel Aviv ahead of similar metropolitan cores in countries of comparable size such as Dublin, Copenhagen, Budapest and Helsinki (Brookings Institution, 2012). Additionally, this data shows that metropolitan cores such as Tel Aviv and Haifa are losing their dominance to their wider metropolitan regions. This diffusion to the wider metropolitan area is pertinent to the case study areas of this study. Just as Tel Aviv's dominance in the national economy has diffused to the Central District over the period 2000-2010, a similar pattern has occurred in the North. The Haifa District has contracted and the Northern District has gained.

However, this has occurred in the context of overall relative decline with respect to the national economy. The Haifa and Northern districts' share of national GDP has contracted from 27.9% to 26.4% over this period (2000-2010). This is contrast to the increasing dominance of the Tel Aviv and Central Districts that grew from 49.3% to 51.1%. This is a significant increase bearing in mind that the Israeli economy grew by about 5% over this period.

Figure 1.2 **Gross regional product as percentage of national GDP, Israel, 2000-2010**

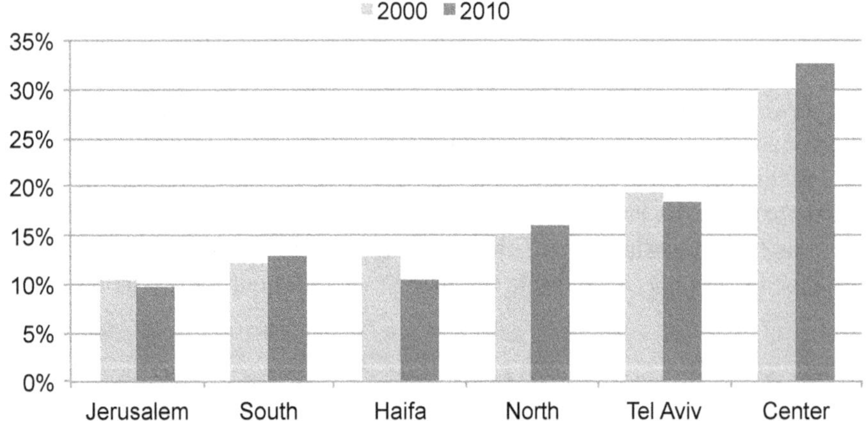

Source: Author's estimate based on CBS data.

Active labour market policy instruments

Israel spends between 0.2%-0.3% of GDP on active labour market policies (ALMPs) which is about half of the OECD average (MOITAL, 2012) (see Figure 1.3). Expanding the employment base is seen as a key factor in reducing inequality and is thus a cornerstone in many active labour market policies in Israel.

Increasing the labour force participation rate has been a major recommendation of two senior level national committees (the Eckstein Committee of 2007 and 2010 and the Trajtenberg Committee in 2012) and was adopted as Government Resolution #1994 in 2010. The government aims to create 700,000 new jobs by 2020. Of these, 300,000 are expected to be created in the Arab sector and a further 180,000 in the Jewish Ultra-Orthodox sector. This means generating employment growth of 175,000 above the rate of natural increase.

To this end, active labour market policies have embraced a series of diverse policy mechanisms aimed at increasing labour force participation such as the "Welfare to Work" programme and the concomitant reduction of allowances to people of working age, the introduction of an earned income tax credit (EITC) for employees, as well as the establishment of Employment Orientation Centres (EOC's) in Arab communities (see Box 1.1). As labour market participation is related to levels of education, increasing participation is also achieved through expanding access to education and training. More needs to be done as the rate of high school graduates who qualify to study at academic institutions is 46.6% in the Jewish population and only 35% in the Arab population (Field and Kuczera 2012).

Box 1.1 Employment Orientation Centres: providing one-stop services for the Arab-Israeli population

Recently, the government has established Employment Orientation Centres (EOCs), which are targeted to the Arab-Israeli population. The centres are managed by the Ministry of the Economy and the Authority for the Economic Development of the Arab Sector within the Prime Minister's office. Seven of a planned 21 centres have been established in minority (Arab, Druze and Bedouin) municipalities, replacing the 'Employment-Promoting City' programme that is being phased out. The case load of the EOCs was 4 000 referrals in 2012. The initiative builds on pilot employment centres established by the JDC-Tevet in recent years in the Arab towns of Tamra and Sakhnin.

The centres aim at creating a one-stop-shop for job seekers offering a comprehensive range of training, placement, vocational guidance, soft skills coaching and re-training services. Employment Orientation Centres provide locally-grounded and individualised services for Arab-Israeli job seekers and the long term unemployed. In contrast to the PES where registration is required in order to qualify for unemployment benefits, registration with an EOC is voluntary.

These centres also engage in partnerships with the local business community and outreach to increase labour force participation rates among disadvantaged groups. The programme is managed by a dedicated NGO called Al-Fanar ('The Lighthouse' in Arabic). This was specially established to ensure the implementation of the programme and ensure Arab leadership and management. The budget for the programme is 220 million NIS.

Figure 1.3 **Expenditure for ALMP as % of GDP, 2011**

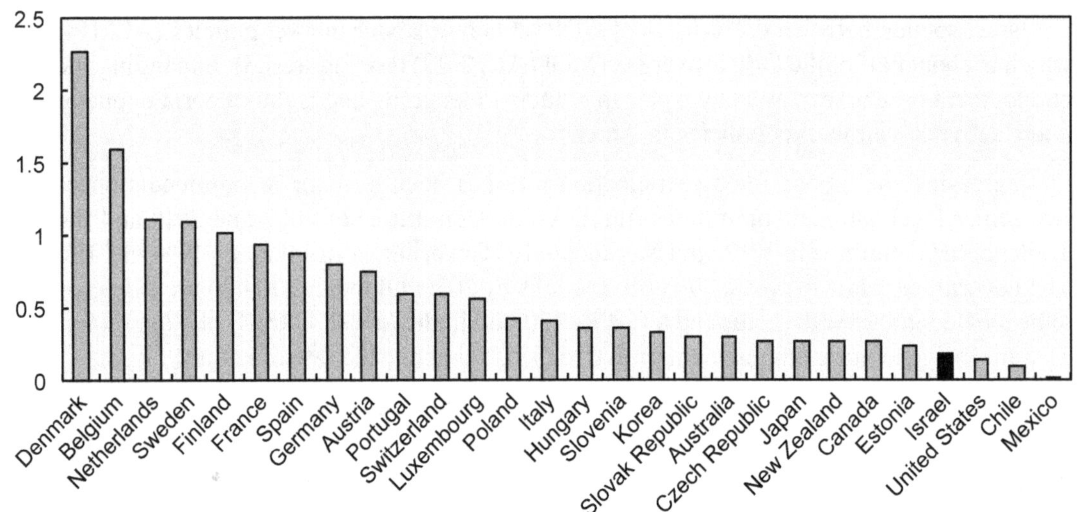

Source: OECD (2013), "Public expenditure on active labour market policies", *Employment and Labour Markets: Key Tables from OECD*, No. 9. doi: http://dx.doi.org/10.1787/lmpxp-table-2013-1-en.

Table 1.1 **Government expenditures on active labour market policies, 2008-2011**

NIS million, 2011 prices

	2008	2009	2010	2011
Vocational Training[a]	618.6	664.1	721.6	732.6
Public Employment Service (PES)	159.2	158.5	162.9	160.6
Encouraging Employment[a]	363.6	390.5	292	303.2
Of which: Welfare to Work	158.1	135.9	84.2	11.8
Of which: Allowance to discharged soldiers[b]	113.6	110.3	125.4	133.5
Encouraging Employment for Immigrants	255.8	243.9	244.1	246.6
Encouraging Employment: people with disabilities	217.4	211.3	244.8	256.8
Entrepreneurship, Small Business etc	31.8	34.0	38.3	40.2
Total	1 646.1	1 702.3	1 703.6	1 740.0
EITC[c]	3.7	89.9	87.1	136.0
Subsidized Childcare[c]	840.3	900.1	951.3	1083.5
Percentage of GDP	0.21	0.21	0.20	0.20
Percentage of budget	0.51	0.52	0.51	0.52

a. Not including programmes for supporting employment of new immigrants and the handicapped.

b. Grant for discharged soldiers working in a preferred job in an industry of national importance.

c. Labour market instruments not included by OECD. Including them raises expenditure on ALMP to 0.3% of GDP.

Source: MOITAL (2012)

The Welfare to Work programme was a large scale comprehensive national labour market policy instrument that operated from 2005-2010 at an annual cost of 300 million NIS. It catered for 46,000 welfare recipients in a variety of low income communities and with histories of chronic unemployment. It succeeded in placing 29,000 welfare recipients in work but only 13,000 of them found long term employment in jobs paying above the national minimum wage.

The programme was never fully implemented across the country and came under severe criticism for adopting a heavy-handed version of the welfare to work model. In addition, it was charged with encouraging the privatisation of the public employment service (PES), linking employment outputs to the cancellation of welfare payments, emphasising job placement and not job quality, lack of transparency and incapable of regulating the proliferation of private manpower service providers. Consequently, it lost political support and was discontinued. It is slated to return in a revised framework, operating within the public employment service, incorporating non-government organisations into its administration and targeting the 'chronically unemployed' (e.g. about 72,000 welfare recipients nationally who have accumulated more than 270 days of unemployment over the last 12 months).

The Earned Income Tax Credit (EITC) is a popular labour market policy instrument that is generally perceived as effective in reducing poverty amongst targeted populations and increasing their labour force participation. It is sometime favoured over other instruments such as minimum wage legislation which raises wages for all low paid workers but does not have any significant effect on unemployment. The EITC carries an opportunity cost as it is a labour market instrument financed entirely by government whereas a minimum wage would be financed by the employer (public or private).

Subsidizing child care is also considered a key labour market instrument in Israel (see Table 1.1 above) for increasing female participation rates. It is considered an important intervention in generating greater 'flexibility' in the female labour force and boosting supply. The female employment rate for ages 25–45 years is 68% while it is 63% among mothers with young children aged 0-4. Based on an employment supply elasticity relative to the cost of care of -0.14, (e.g. a 1% decrease in childcare costs leading to an increase in female participation of 4%), the Bank of Israel has estimated that raising female participation from 63% to 67% (an additional 27,000 women) would cost 135 000 NIS per new employee (Bank of Israel, 2011).

Mapping the institutional framework for employment and skills

Israel is a small and highly centralised country with a strong national government. While the country is divided into six administrative regions (districts), these are hardly independent regional economies or even self-contained labour markets. Consequently it is hard to define a regional strata of governance or economic activity. In principle, local authorities are sovereign representatives of local interests. However in terms of local employment and economic development activities, their perspective is limited and non-strategic. They view economic activity in terms of short term property tax income as key to fiscal autonomy. Issues of welfare, the distribution of the quality and nature of jobs and employment mobility are not on their agendas. As a result, the majority of strategic activity for employment and economic development activities is carried out by national agencies operating locally.

Figure 1.4 divides employment and economic activity into three spheres: 1) labour market policy, 2) skills development; and 3) economic development. These are not exclusive categories that exist at both the national and local levels and can be provided by different stakeholders in the public, private and NGO sectors.

The Ministry of Economy (MOE) is responsible for labour market policy, including skills development and job placement activities. Service delivery of much of these programmes managed by the Ministry of Economy takes place at the local level through regional offices. Other stakeholders involved in labour market policy include the Prime Minister's Office via the Authority for the Economic Development of the Arab Sector (AEDA), the Ministry of Welfare (MOW), the Ministry of Finance (MOF), the Ministry of Education (MED), Ministry of Immigrant Absorption (MIA), the Local Authorities (LAs), various non-Governmental Organisations (NGOs) and the private sector through its role as an employer.

The Public Employment Service (PES) is a statutory authority mandated under the National Employment Service law of 1959 and operates under the aegis of the Ministry of Economy. In addition to administrating unemployment benefits, it operates placement and matching services. It also offers vocational assessment, guidance and placement for the unemployed and other job seekers who legally qualify for its services. There are 70 field offices nationally with a caseload of around 500,000 individuals annually. It also offers training for those in need of coaching or seeking re-entry into the labour force with several workshops catering for about 5 000 job seekers. The PES maintains a data base and on-line information system of all of the clients it has served and of all jobs on offer until filled.

Vocational education and training is managed primarily via the Manpower Training and Development Bureau (MTDB) at the Ministry of Economy. It operates roughly 500 vocational courses annually catering for 7 500 people. The MTDB offers vouchers that cover the cost of training offered by recognised institutions (public and private). These are available to roughly 1 500 recipients annually. Both the PES and the EOC's utilise the courses and services offered by the MTDB. Occupational certifications are managed by the Ministry of Economy in more than 100 different professions with 211 basic certifications and 76 upgraded ones. Some 70 000 people take these examinations each year, sometimes at the end of an educational programme, sometimes as a stand-alone examination. There are 14 different areas of training and some 80 subjects of study available within industrial schools and schools for apprentices, however, only 3% among upper-secondary students (Musset, P., M. Kuczera and S. Field, 2014).

In parallel, the Authority for the Economic Development of the Arab Sector within the Prime Minister's office has a suite of programmes targeted to the Arab-Israeli population. As a targeted government agency, it offers similar interventions that are available generally but in a more culturally-friendly environment. In the area of employment it brokers existing government initiatives to the Arab population. Thus it offers training via the Ministry of Economy's funded voucher programme. It offers a direct employment subsidy to employers (25% of wages in general sectors, 40% in high tech) via incentives provided by the Investment Centre of the Ministry of Economy. It partners with the private sector (for example, the Kav Mashveh NGO) in offering placement services for Arab academics. Aside from its policy and budgetary role, the AEDA co-ordinates between the government and various stakeholders in the Arab sector: such as employers, NGO's and local government.

Figure 1.4 **Institutional framework for employment, skills, and economic development policies**

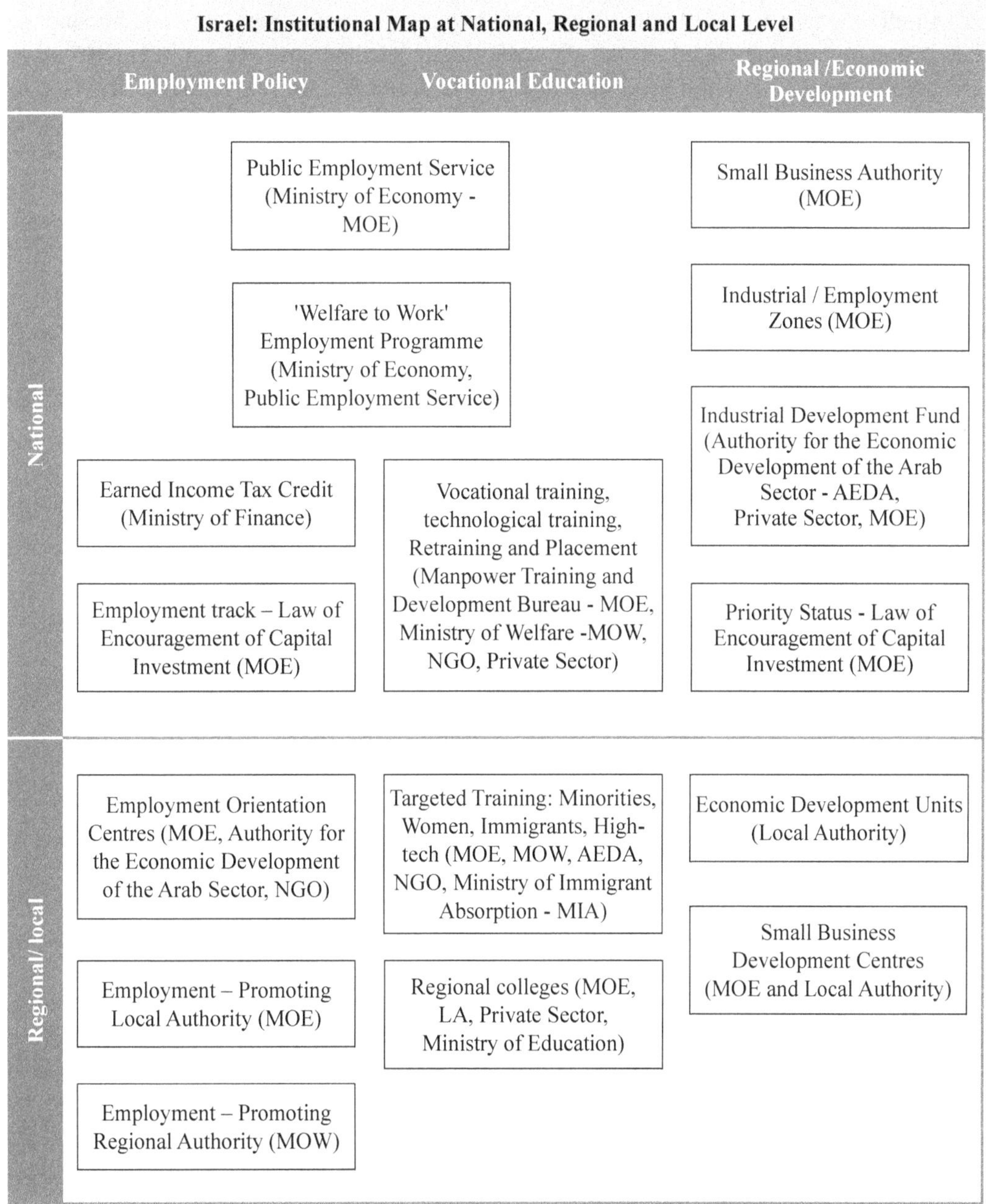

The Ministry of Economy also operates a Small Business Authority (SBA), which provides assistance ranging from courses for teaching entrepreneurial skills, establishing small business centres that offer subsidised office space through to small business loan funds and public-private equity investment funds. The Authority for the Economic Development of the Arab Sector within the Prime Minister's office also has business tools are also close to those offered by the SBA such as a joint government-private equity fund for encouraging investment, a small business loan fund, as well as micro finance and subsidised business centres.

In terms of local economic development, local authorities are a fairly weak governance tier and do not undertake much strategic activity. Some small business development centres are funded in part by local authorities. The larger local authorities may have economic development units mandated to take a more strategic local perspective but in practice, they are involved either in land development or other property tax- related activities such as zoning. For example, the attraction of large external investments to a locality (for example, the case of the Intel fabrication plant in Kiryat Gat) is generally handled by the Ministry of Economy or the Ministry of Finance. The local authority is invariably bypassed in the decision making process. Any incentives offered will come from the central government. Local government in Israel has no authority to induce investment for example, via local tax breaks.

The role of the Ministry of Welfare (MOW) as an institutional stakeholder should also be noted. While traditionally engaged in providing services to populations with physical and emotional disabilities, this government agency has extended its services to employment placement of populations generally experiencing social distress. It emphasises community building and has extended the traditional role of the social worker to that of employment broker and has advocated increasing labour market participation as a strategy for empowering disadvantaged population groups.

Constraints to increased labour market participation of the Arab-Israeli Minority

A key focus of this study is looking at policies which have been targeted to support job creation as well as economic and inclusive growth of minority groups in Israel – in particular Arab-Israelis. A number of studies have examined the constraints to their labour market participation, which include a number of structural factors (OECD 2010; Yashiv, 2013b). These include:

Structural Barriers: One of the main barriers to labour force participation for Arab-Israelis is the requirement for proficiency in English and Hebrew. Consequently, the Arab labour force needs to be tri-lingual in order to improve their labour market success. This barrier is often compounded with other demographic and cultural constraints such as large average family sizes that limit the participation of women and a reticence to participate in the labour market due to the absence of soft employment skills. For Arab men, concentration in low level manual labour and the concomitant declining physical ability to undertake heavy labour with age are structural barriers compounded by insufficient access to education and training opportunities. For Arab women, low level labour market aspirations due to traditional family-community commitments represent a barrier enforced by cultural norms.

Ethnicity Barriers: These are often expressed as employer discrimination in hiring and wage arrangements, which are further compounded by low educational levels. Arab employment and wages are low because of low educational levels and education is low because of the low level of earnings and work experience. Discrimination is often offered as an explanation when residual gaps in employment and wages persist after controlling for all socio-economic attributes such as background, family situation and place of residence. This ethnic wage and employment gap is especially an issue with respect to male (under-employed) Arab university graduates.

Cultural Barriers: Traditionally socio-cultural norms have viewed female Arab employment as a means for generating additional household income but not an end of itself. This means that female career development is not valued and is accompanied by low expectations of well-paid employment. Women's employment is consequently constrained to those sectors considered suitable for combining household responsibilities and employment which limits the employment opportunities available (e.g. particularly low skilled and part time work). This results in a number of Arab-Israeli females employed in child care, personal services and para-medical occupations, which are generally low quality jobs.

Globalisation Barriers: A number of good paying jobs are found within the ICT and high-tech sectors, which require higher levels of education and work experience. Exposure to these occupations often comes through the Israeli military system which is not open to the Arab population. At the other end of the labour market, traditional labour intensive sectors are declining resulting in diminishing job opportunities. The global shift in traditional manufacturing sectors such as textiles has caused many Israeli companies to out-source their production. This has negatively impacted the small scale factories that exist in Arab villages within Israel. Global trends towards larger scale production have also caused the Arab-Israeli SME sector to decline in its overall contribution to economic activity.

Spatial and infrastructural barriers: The spatial separation between Jews and Arabs means that social networks that often go with finding a job are not developed across the two population groups. Another spatial factor is the lack of regular bussing or worker transportation facilities that makes working outside the community non-viable especially for Arab women. A lack of adequate child care facilities is another supply side bottleneck that inherently constrains female participation. Finally, the Arab population distribution is dispersed across many small and impoverished local authorities mainly located in the north and south of the country and generally located outside the economic nexus of the Tel Aviv/Central districts.

Impact of the Israeli Arab Conflict: This is a pervasive issue that affects job opportunities, education and training opportunities. As Arab-Israelis are not allowed to serve in the military, they are not exposed to the cutting edge technology, which requires a higher level of skills and training, improving chances of labour success. They also do not develop the social networks that army service affords and that assist in employment placement. Furthermore, intense violence (such as the first and second intifadas) have resulted in negative economic shocks within some Israeli-Arab communities, such as the decline in tourism in Nazareth as well as more pervasive effects such as the layoff of many Israeli-Arab workers by Jewish employers.

References

Ben-David D (2012) (ed.), *State of the Nation Report, Society, Economy and Policy in Israel 2011-12*, Taub Center for Social Policy Studies, Jerusalem.

BOI (2011), *Annual Report 2011*, Bank of Israel, Jerusalem.

Brookings Institution (2012), *Global Metro Monitor 2012*, Metropolitan Policy Program, Brookings Institution, Washington DC.

Field S and Kuczera M (2012), *A Skills Beyond School Commentary on Israel*, OECD Reviews of Vocational Education and Training, Paris.

MOITAL (2012), *Progress Report on the Implementation of the OECD Recommendations: Labour Market and Social Policies*, Israel, Ministry of Industry, Trade and Labor, Jerusalem.

Musset, P., M. Kuczera and S. Field (2014), *A Skills beyond School Review of Israel*, OECD Reviews of Vocational Education and Training, OECD Publishing, Paris. DOI: *http://dx.doi.org/10.1787/9789264210769-en*

OECD (2014), *Education at a Glance 2014: OECD Indicators: Israel Country Note*, *www.oecd.org/edu/Israel-EAG2014-Country-Note.pdf*

OECD (2013a), *OECD Economic Surveys: Israel 2013*, OECD Publishing, Paris. DOI: *http://dx.doi.org/10.1787/eco_surveys-isr-2013-en*

OECD (2013b), *Review of Recent Developments and Progress in Labour Market and Social Policy in Israel: Slow Progress Towards a More Inclusive Society*, OECD Publishing, Paris. DOI: *http://dx.doi.org/10.1787/9789264200401-en*

OECD (2011), *Study on the Geographic Coverage of Israeli Data*, OECD Statistics Directorate, OECD, Paris, *www.oecd.org/els/48442642.pdf*

OECD (2010), *OECD Reviews of Labour Market and Social Policies: Israel*, OECD Publishing, Paris. DOI: *http://dx.doi.org/10.1787/9789264079267-en*

Yashiv, E. and N. Kasir (2013a), Arab Women in the Israeli Labor Market: Characteristics and Policy Proposals, *Israel Economic Review*, 10 (2),.1-41.

Yashiv, E. and N. Kasir (2013b), *The Labor Market for Arab Israelis: Characteristics and Policy Choices*, Department of Public Policy, Tel Aviv University, *www.tau.ac.il/~yashiv/IsraeliArabs_policy_paper.pdf*

Yashiv, E. and N. Kasir (2011), Patterns of Labor Force Participation Among Israeli Arabs, *Israel Economic Review*, 9 (1),. 53-101.

Chapter 2

Overview of the Israel case study areas*

To better understand the role of the local level in contributing to job creation and productivity, this review examined policy and programme activities in two regions: 1) Haifa; and 2) Yizreel. This chapter provides a labour market and economic overview of each region as well as the results from an OECD LEED statistical tool which looks at the relationship between skills supply and demand at the sub-national level. Both areas have different local economies and labour market characteristics.

* The statistical data for Israel are supplied by and under the responsibility of the relevant Israeli authorities. The use of such data by the OECD is without prejudice to the status of the Golan Heights, East Jerusalem and Israeli settlements in the West Bank under the terms of international law.

Overview of the case study regions

The two case study areas analysed for this study are contiguous sub-districts running from west to east across northern Israel (see Figure 2.1). While these sub-districts are arbitrarily defined administrative areas, the Haifa area has some functional logic. It is comprised of the core and inner ring of the Haifa metropolitan area and can therefore be considered an economic entity roughly corresponding to a housing and labour (commuting) market. The total population of the Haifa sub district is 549,000 with over nearly 50% living in the city of Haifa and another 34% in its satellite communities (see Annex A).

Figure 2.1 **Overview of case study areas**

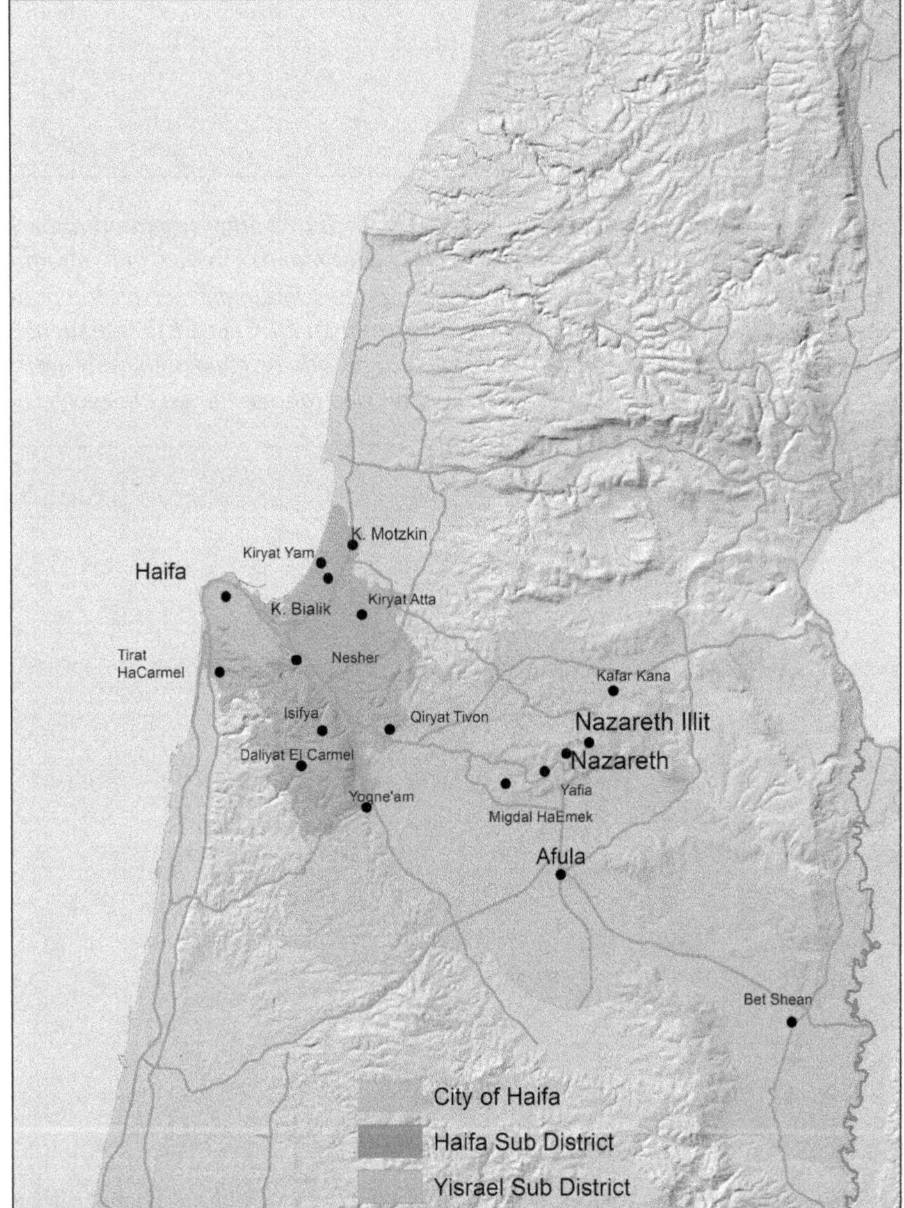

Source: Map compiled by author.

The composition of the population is primarily Jewish but there are large non-Jewish communities existing in the city of Haifa whose Arab community is about 60,000 and in the Druze town of Dalit El Carmel (16,000) and surrounding villages. In total, Jews comprise 80% of the sub district and Arabs and Druze represent 10% respectively.

In contrast, the Yizreel sub district is a more artificial creation with a more heterogeneous population. It includes 23 small towns and villages across a diverse terrain and cannot be considered a uniform region functionally or geographically. While the Central Bureau of Statistics (CBS) considers this one sub district, the Ministry of the Interior divides the area into two separate units: one centred on the Arab city of Nazareth (with a population of 74,000) and its satellite communities and the other centred on the Jewish city of Afula (with a population of 42,000) and its hinterland comprised of Jewish and Bedouin communities. The total population of the Yizreel sub district is 452,000 of which 56% are Arabs and 44% are Jews.

Labour force trends across the case study areas

Local level data published by the Central Bureau of Statistics (CBS) allows comparisons of labour market performance across sub district levels. The following key variables are available from 2000 to 2011:

- earnings;
- labour market participation (including unemployment rate);
- labour force mismatch (job search, commuting); and
- employment in economic branches stratified by socio-demographic characteristics (nationality, sex).

These data are also aggregated to create regional (sub-district) averages or proportions. The regional aggregates are stratified by key socio-economic variables such as ethnicity (Jewish/Arab) and sex (male/female). Table 2.1 shows the key economic and labour market trends of the Haifa and Yizreel sub-districts compared to the national average. One can see quite clearly that the Haifa sub district reflects and even exceeds the national average with respect to income, education and unemployment. With respect to education, as well as years of schooling, Haifa performs better than the national average.

In contrast, the Yizreel sub district has lower levels of education and a higher share of less educated people than the national average and is much lower than Haifa on these variables. It also has a higher average level of unemployment and less people actively looking for work than either Haifa or the national average. However, labour market participation rates are similar to those of Haifa and the national average.

The Haifa sub district is dominated by the Haifa metropolitan area and this is reflected in the labour market variables related to commuting and local job opportunities. In contrast, the Yizreel sub district comprises a heterogeneous collection of both Jewish and Arab small communities. Nazereth is the largest town in the area and serves as an economic centre for the Arab villages in its hinterland. However it does not serve the Jewish small towns some of whom are in the orbit of the Haifa metropolitan area and others (such as Bet Shean) which serve as regional service centres for the rural communities that surround them. As such, the Yizreel sub district does not function as an economic region nor does it represent any distinct self-contained travel to work area. Some of the variables listed in Table 2.1 have been further utilised to estimate wages and labour participation models (see Annex D for full regression results).

Table 2.1 **Key economic and labour market outcomes across the case study areas, 2011**

Variable	Level	National	Haifa	Yizreel
Earnings*	Average (monthly, Nominal NIS)	8563	9544	6574
Sex	Male	48.8%	47.7%	49.5%
	Female	51.2%	52.3%	50.5%
Nationality	Jewish	79.9%	87.0%	76.2%
	Arab	17.9%	9.8%	22.8%
	other	2.2%	3.1%	1.1%
Avg Schooling	Years	13.3	13.4	12.6
Job Search	weeks	1.1	1.2	1.7
Unemployment rate		5.6%	5.6%	6.4%
Labour force composition	Labour force	57.4%	58.0%	58.5%
	Inactive population	42.6%	42.0%	41.5%
Commuting	work in locality of residence	48.3%	51.6%	45.1%
	work outside locality of residence	45.7%	41.3%	45.9%
	work in different places	6.1%	7.1%	9.0%
Actively Looked for Job in Past Year	yes	3.5%	3.2%	2.6%
	no	96.5%	96.8%	97.4%
Schooling	1-8 Years	8.0%	6.8%	9.0%
	16+years	21.6%	23.1%	16.4%

Source: National Insurance Institute, 2010

Earnings

Average nominal monthly wages are trending upwards both nationally and in the study areas. In both areas, wages grew at a rapid rate from 1990-2002 (5% annually) and continued to grow at a slower rate (2-3% annually) from 2000 onwards (see Figures 5.1 and 5.2 in Annex C for more information). Haifa and national trends are similar while wage levels in Yizreel are lower for both male and females. When stratifying by location, trends are almost identical with average women's wages about 30% lower irrespective of location. From 2000-2011, wages for Jews and Arabs seem to have diverged in both Yizreel and Haifa. Arab wages pull down the average wages in both the Haifa and Yizreel sub districts. Thus wages in Yizreel are substantially lower than in Haifa. The latter is very close to and even slightly exceeds the national average. The wage gaps between Jews and Arabs in each sub district seem to have diverged slightly over a 20 year period.

Labour force participation

Labour force participation rates in Israel have grown nationally over the last decade to around 63.5% in 2012. However once this is stratified by ethnicity and gender, the sectoral nuances hidden by this trend become clear. Arab female participation rates are around 25-30% and much lower than their Jewish counterparts. This situation is even more pronounced in the Yizreel sub district where Arab female participation is around 20%. In contrast, Arab male participation is higher (over 60%) and much more equal to the Jewish population (see Figures 5.3 and 5.4 in Annex C for more information).

While labour participation rates among the prime working group (24-65 years) are on a par with the OECD average of 78%, highlighting particular sensitive age classes at the beginning and the end of the age spectrum reveals a rather different picture. The Arab youth participation rate is lower than for their Jewish counterparts despite the fact that the data for Jewish participation discounts all those in the national service and relates only to the civilian labour force participation.

In Haifa, the Arab youth labour force participation rate has exceeded and fallen short of Jewish youth over time. In Yizreel and nationally, youth labour force participation consistently falls below the Jewish rates (see Figure 5.5 in Annex C for more information on trends in youth unemployment). At the other end of the age continuum (50+), unemployment among Arab older workers is consistently below the Jewish rate of around 50% (see Figure 5.6 in Annex C for more information). While they have slowly increased over the past decade, they are still much lower than the Jewish rates for this age group and do not surpass 25% in Yizreel and 30% in Haifa. While the trend nationally is towards greater participation of older populations in the labour force, a corresponding pattern is not easily discernible for Arab-Israelis. Together with the increase in life expectancy and the decreasing physical capabilities of manual labour in which the Arab-Israeli population is over-represented, this raises serious concerns with the respect to welfare benefits and pension system adequacy for an ageing Arab population.

Unemployment

Despite the global economic crisis, unemployment has contracted over the last decade from around 10% to 7%. This low level has been attributed to structural changes such as increases in education and an emphasis on labour market flexibility including stricter unemployment insurance criteria, more temporary employment and labour turnover, streamlining job search processes and out-sourcing placement and training to the private sector (Habib et al, 2010). While male and female unemployment rates nationally have remained close, when further sub-dividing by nationality, large divergences become apparent. For the sub-districts, Arab female unemployment is higher and more volatile than the Jewish unemployment rate reaching over 20% in Yizreel from 2000-2010. In contrast, a comparison of Arab and Jewish male unemployment shows a similar pattern of declining trends over time with Arab unemployment marginally above Jewish unemployment in all regions (see Figures 5.7 and 5.8 in Annex C for more information).

Youth unemployment has traditionally been about 20-25% nationally and exhibits a declining trend over time. These rates are much lower than corresponding EU rates (OECD 2012). The two case study areas exhibit higher rates than the national average and youth unemployment among Jews is consistently higher than its Arab counterpart (see Figure 5.9

in Annex C). These counter-intuitive findings may be due to the fact that military service amongst the Jewish population reduces the pool from which unemployment shares are calculated thereby inflating the share of Jewish youth not in the army and registered as unemployed. Unemployment rates of older workers in both sub districts are higher than the national average. In the Yizreel area, these rates have been over 10% higher for Arab senior workers than for Jews.

Labour market matching

We present two variables relating to labour market matching. The first refers to the proportion of the population actively looking for employment over the previous 4 weeks. An interesting distinction is apparent between the Arab female and male populations. Arab female job search has declined over the second half of the last decade both nationally and in the sub-districts. Male active job search in contrast has increased. The proportion of Arab male and female job seekers is consistently above that of their Jewish counterparts due to higher levels of unemployment and lower participation rates. For both Jewish males and females, the proportion of active job seekers over the last decade has been around 2%. In contrast, for Arab job seekers, this proportion has risen to 6-8% in certain periods.

The second variable relates to geographical mismatch as represented by those working outside their place of residence. We compare Jewish and Arab labour commuting patterns in the study areas in order to observe where mismatches could be occurring. While the tendency to work locally is similar across Jews and Arabs in Haifa, in Yizreel the difference between the two populations is much more pronounced. 40% of Jews work locally while the proportion of Arabs is about 20% in Yizreel and 25-30% nationally. If the need to work outside of locality of residence reflects a limited supply of suitable jobs locally, then this mismatch would seem to affect the Arab workers in local labour markets more than Jewish workers (see Figures 5.11 and 5.12 in Annex C).

Education

Given the relationship between education and labour market participation, we highlight the least and most educated segments of the labour market over time. The gaps are most acute with respect to Arab females with low levels of education. Their share of all educated is constantly higher than that of their Jewish counterparts. This is the situation nationally and in the study areas and is most pronounced in the Yizreel sub-district. As expected, when looking at the share of highly educated females in the Arab sector (e.g. 16+ years of schooling), their share is lower than that of the low education group. It is consistently under half that of their Jewish counterparts both nationally and across the case study areas.

In the case of differences between males in both the low and high education groups, the patterns of difference between Jews and Arabs are similar to those of females, but less accentuated. At the low end, Arab males are a higher proportion of the labour force than Jewish males and nationally the trends seem to be slightly converging. At the highest levels, Jewish males form a larger share of the educated workforce than highly educated Arabs and these differences seem be diverging slightly over time (see Figures 5.13 and 5.14 in Annex C).

Economic branches

Labour force participation obviously varies by economic branches as different sub-populations display differing degrees of accessibility to occupations. Here we highlight some of these differences for select branches emphasising those that have distinct gender and national identities. We look at economic activities and contrast Jewish-Arab male occupational patterns in the case study areas. These are construction, manufacturing, agriculture and retail trade. For the female labour force we look at education, health, as well as manufacturing and retail trade.

In the construction industry Arab males represent a large proportion of the labour supply. The share of Arab males in this group who are residents of the Yizreel sub district is greater than the national average while in Haifa their representation is under the national average. Retail trade has a similar pattern to construction but a major difference between them is that the former is ubiquitous whereas employment in the latter is concentrated within select regions. As such, the likelihood of mismatches is much greater in construction than in retail trade.

Education and health care are two occupations associated with Arab female employment. In the case of the former, the national and local concentrations of Arab women are readily apparent. With respect to health care, while the national proportions are very similar, at the sub district level, things are more volatile. In Yizreel, over the period 2002-2007 the proportion of Arab women in health occupations is very high but then dropped dramatically thereafter. In manufacturing, Jewish and Arab women are employed in roughly equal shares both nationally and in Haifa. Contrastingly, in Yizreel the share of Jewish women in industrial occupations is almost double that of Arabs.

Regression analysis of wages and participation rate

We now attempt to explain the factors behind the observed difference in wages and labour market participation rates across the study areas. We use panel data regression and Table 6.1 in Annex D presents both a wages model (Columns 1 and 2) and a labour participation model (cols 3-7).

The wage model comprises 17 panels for three cross sections (Haifa, Yizreel and National) for a total of 51 observations over the period 1995-2011. The model is estimated separately for males and females. The dependent variable is wage growth (year on year change in wages) and the estimation procedure is panel data regression with fixed effects. The variables are all in logs and thus the coefficients can be interpreted as elasticities.

The labour participation model has separate estimations for males/females and Jews/Arabs. The panel here comprises 21 periods (1991-2011) for three cross-sections giving 63 observations. The dependent variable is growth (year on year change) in labour force participation.

Both models use fixed effects (FE) to control for time invariant characteristics that may impact or bias the predictor variables. They remove the effect of these characteristics from the predictor variables so that their net effect can be assessed. Fixed effects also assume that the model errors are not correlated (e.g. the time-invariant characteristics are unique and are not correlated with other characteristics). The models include fixed effects for the influence of national characteristics and for those related to Haifa or Yizreel.

For the wages model, we expect growth in wages to be positively related to growth in both education and the labour force participation rate and inversely related to length of job search and age. Most of the coefficients display the 'correct' signs and are significant but the model is weak overall. Significantly, growth of one extra week spent job searching reduces monthly wages by 7-9%. Counter-intuitively, the results suggest that growth in labour force participation places downward pressure on male's wages. This may be due to growth in the size of the labour pool.

Fixed effects are small and consistently negative for Haifa and the national level but positive for Yizreel. The Durbin-Watson (DW) statistic is generally used to identify the presence of autocorrelation in the residuals. Given the panel model estimation, it is used here to test for co-integration between the variables. The critical value of DW lies between 0 and 4.0. If DW is substantially less than 2.0, this suggests serial correlation. In our case, the DW is slightly under 2.0 not strongly suggesting that this is an issue.

We anticipate that growth in participation will be positively related to education and to working locally and inversely related to age. This model has five variants that are all roughly consistent suggesting a more robust estimation than for wages. The results show that education increases labour market participation but more for women than for men and more for Arabs than for Jews. Age is inversely related to participation as expected.

The results also indicate the adverse impacts of potential skills mismatches as it relates to the effect of working outside the locality of residence. Increasing local working has a positive and significant effect on labour force participation in all models. Increasing non-commuting (e.g. working locally) by 1% leads to 5% growth in Arab labour market participation and 3% growth in female Arab labour market participation. The DW statistics for all models indicate there is no issue of serial correlation. The characteristics of the Haifa and national labour markets have a small but positive effect of growth in labour market participation while in most cases Yizreel has the opposite effect.

Balance between skills supply and demand at the sub-national level

To supplement the above analysis, the OECD LEED Programme has developed a statistical tool to understand the balance between skills supply and demand within local labour markets (Froy, Giguère and Meghnagi, 2012). In the Israeli context, this tool can supplement the previous analysis to provide policy makers with an understanding of potential skills mismatches, which may be occurring at the sub-national level. It can also inform place-based policy approaches at the local level.

Figure 2.2 **Understanding the relationship between skills supply and demand**

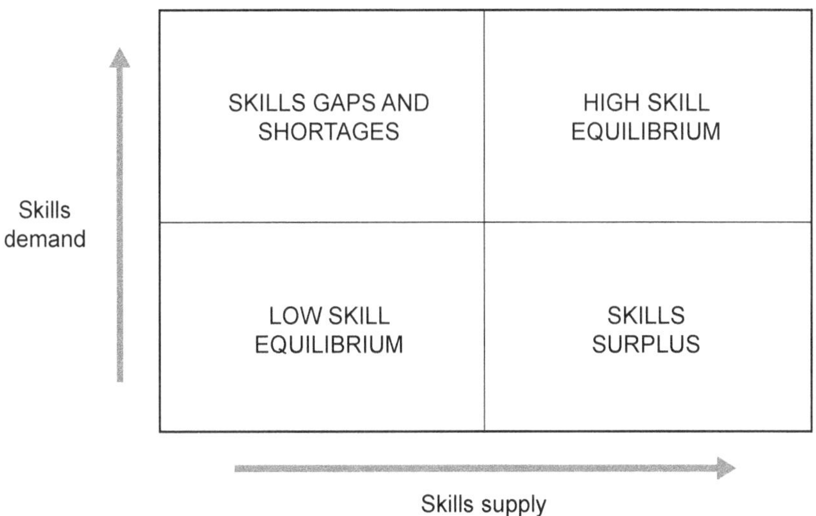

Source: Froy, F. and S. Giguère (2010), "Putting in Place Jobs that Last: A Guide to Rebuilding Quality Employment at Local Level" , OECD Local Economic and Employment Development (LEED) Working Papers, No. 2010/13, OECD Publishing. doi: *http://dx.doi.org/10.1787/5km7jf7qtk9p-en*

Looking at the figure above, in the top-left corner (skills gaps and shortages), demand for high skills is met by a supply of low skills, a situation that results in reported skills gaps and shortages. In the top-right corner, demand for high skills is met by an equal supply of high skills resulting in a high-skill equilibrium. This is the most desired destination of all high performing local economies. At the bottom-left corner the demand for low skills is met by a supply of low skills resulting in a low-skill equilibrium. The challenge facing policymakers is to get the economy moving in a north-easterly direction towards the top-right corner. Lastly, in the bottom-right corner, demand for low skills is met by a supply of high skills resulting in an economy where what high skills are available are not utilised. This leads to the out migration of talent, underemployment, skill under-utilisation, and attrition of human capital, all of which signal missed opportunities for creating prosperity.

Box 2.2 **Explaining the diagnostic tool**

The analysis is carried out at Territorial Level 3 regions (regions with populations ranging between 150 000-800 000). The supply of skills was measured by the percentage of the population with post-secondary education. The demand for skills was measured by the percentage of the population employed in medium-high skilled occupations. Regions are also classified in relation to the average state unemployment rate. The indices are standardised using the inter-decile method and are compared with the national median. Further explanations on the methodology can be found in Froy, Giguère and Meghnagi, 2012.

Source: Froy, F., S. Giguère and M. Meghnagi (2012), "Skills for Competitiveness: A Synthesis Report", OECD Local Economic and Employment Development (LEED) Working Papers, No. 2012/09, OECD Publishing. doi: *http://dx.doi.org/10.1787/5k98xwskmvr6-en*

Figure 2.3 **Balancing skills supply and demand in Israel, 2005**

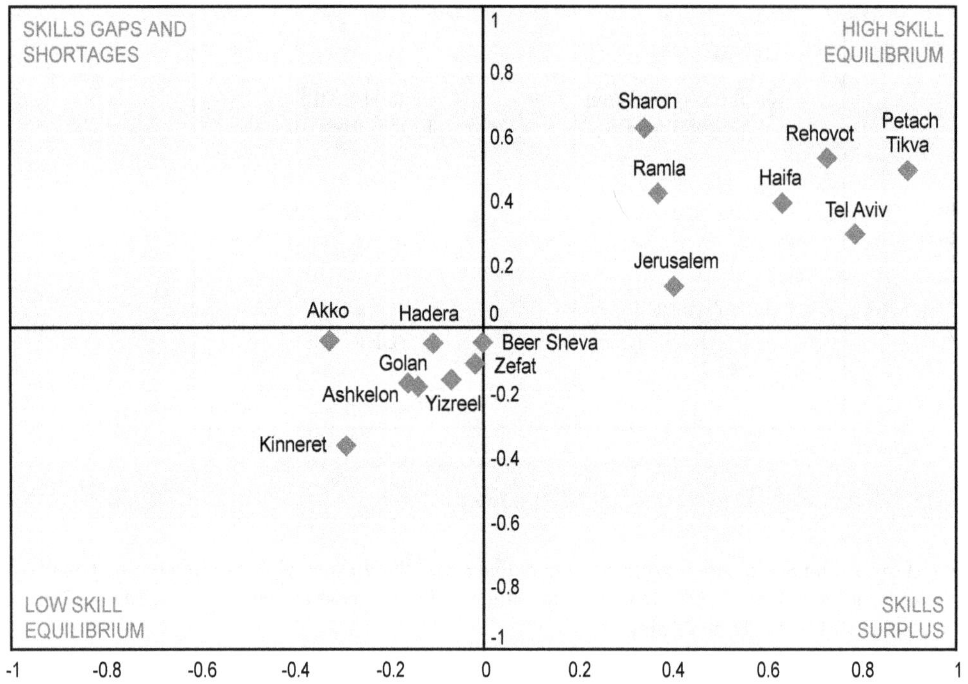

SKILLS GAPS AND
SHORTAGES
HIGH SKILL
EQUILIBRIUM
LOW SKILL
EQUILIBRIUM
SKILLS
SURPLUS
Sharon
Rehovot
Petach
Tikva
Ramla
Haifa
Tel Aviv
Jerusalem
Akko
Hadera
Beer Sheva
Golan
Zefat
Ashkelon
Yizreel
Kinneret
1
0.8
0.6
0.4
0.2
0
-0.2
-0.4
-0.6
-0.8
-1
-1
-0.8
-0.6
-0.4
-0.2
0
0.2
0.4
0.6
0.8
1

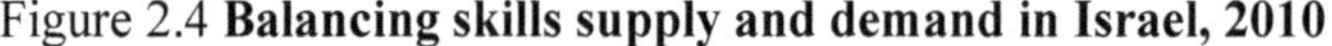

Figure 2.4 **Balancing skills supply and demand in Israel, 2010**

SKILLS GAPS AND
SHORTAGES
HIGH SKILL
EQUILIBRIUM
LOW SKILL
EQUILIBRIUM
SKILLS
SURPLUS
Sharon
Rehovot
Petach Tikva
Ramla
Tel Aviv
Haifa
Akko
Hadera
Jerusalem
Yizreel
Ashkelon
Beer Sheva
Golan
Zefat
Kinneret
1
0.8
0.6
0.4
0.2
0
-0.2
-0.4
-0.6
-0.8
-1
-1
-0.8
-0.6
-0.4
-0.2
0
0.2
0.4
0.6
0.8
1

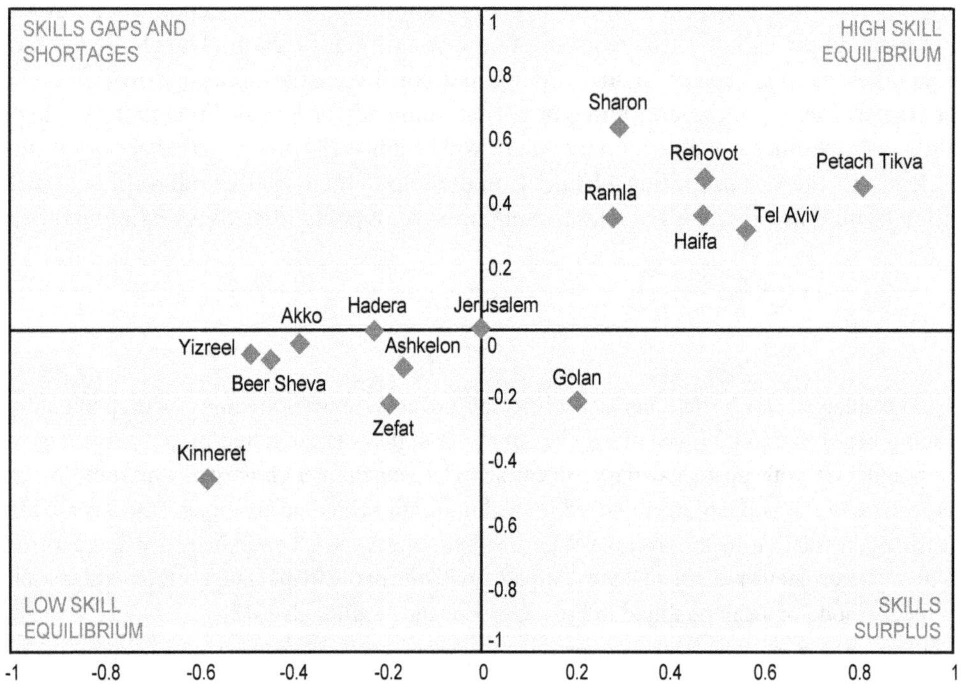

This typology is applied to the 16 sub-districts in Israel (Figs 2.3 and 2.4). The two areas of interest display different trajectories over the period 2005-2010. The Haifa sub-district is broadly stable located in the high skill equilibrium quadrant with only a slight symmetric decline in both supply and demand for skilled labour over the study period. In contrast, the Yizreel sub-district presents a less consistent picture. While demand for skills has remained constant, supply capacity has declined suggesting a supply-demand mis-match and an increasing lock-in at a low-skill equilibrium.

Conclusions

The case study areas are geographically contiguous but very different in terms of their labour market processes. The empirical data presented above underscores these differences. The Haifa sub district is dominated by the employment opportunities offered by the city of Haifa and its satellites. Consequently, it offers higher earnings to a more educated labour force than Yizreel. The latter is a much more heterogeneous area with no distinct focal point and some small urban centres that have yet to reach a critical mass (e.g. Nazereth Illit, Afula and Nazareth). Haifa is classified as a high skills equilibrium region which has remained constant from 2005-2010. In contrast, Yizreel is classified as a low skills equilibrium region, which indicates a prevalence of low quality jobs and a loss of skilled people relative to the rest of the country. This results in more non-local employment and inter-district commuting for the Arab population of the towns and villages of the area. In contrast to Haifa, the Yizreel sub-district is hardly a self-contained labour market. Our analytic findings point to increasing labour force participation rates as having a positive effect on non-commuting patterns (i.e. working locally) especially amongst Arab and female workers.

The labour market trends of the two sub districts suggests some interesting issues in terms of what might be appropriate in each area. Increasing employment participation offers two broad approaches. The first is acquiring greater skills that lead to greater mobility and employment. In the case of the Haifa sub district, this would seem to be the natural trajectory. For Yizreel this would lead to integration with the national labour market but would also mean a cost in terms of wider job search, greater commuting distances and the need for encouraging local economic development initiatives.

References

Habib J., King J., Ben Shoham A, Wolde-Tsadick A and Lasky K (2010), *Labor Market and Socio Economic Outcomes of the Arab-Israeli Population*, OECD Social Employment and Migration Working Papers No 102, OECD, Paris. DOI: *http://dx.doi.org/10.1787/5kmjnrcfsskc-en*

OECD (2012), *Local Job Creation: How Employment and Training Agencies Can Help*, Programme on Local Economic and Employment Development (LEED), Paris.

Chapter 3

Local job creation dashboard findings in Israel*

This chapter highlights findings from the OECD local job creation dashboard in Israel. The findings are discussed through the four thematic areas of the review: 1) better aligning policies and programmes to local employment development; 2) adding value through skills; 3) targeting policy to local employment sectors and investing in quality jobs; and 4) being inclusive.

* The statistical data for Israel are supplied by and under the responsibility of the relevant Israeli authorities. The use of such data by the OECD is without prejudice to the status of the Golan Heights, East Jerusalem and Israeli settlements in the West Bank under the terms of international law.

Results from the dashboard

This section of the report presents the key findings from the in-depth fieldwork undertaken in Israel. Figure 3.1 shows the overall results from the OECD local job creation dashboard across the four thematic areas of the review. In this chapter, each of the four priority areas within each theme is presented and discussed sequentially, accompanied by an explanation of the results.

Figure 3.1. **Local job creation dashboard results for Israel**

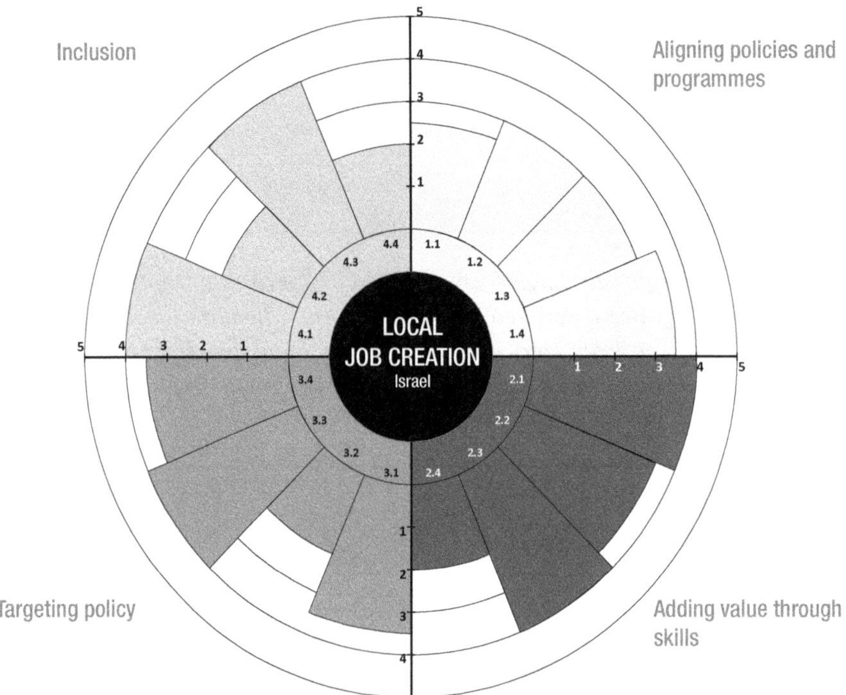

Theme 1: Better aligning policy and programmes to local economic development

Flexibility in the delivery of employment and vocational training policies

The OECD defines flexibility as 'the possibility to adjust policy at its various design, implementation and delivery stages to make it better adapted to local contexts, actions carried out by other organisations, strategies being pursued, and challenges and opportunities faced' (Giguère and Froy, 2009). Flexibility deals with the latitude that exists in the management of the employment system, rather than the flexibility in the labour market itself. The achievement of local flexibility does not necessarily mean that governments need to politically decentralise (Giguère and Froy, 2009). Governments just need to give sufficient latitude when allocating responsibilities in the fields of designing policies and programmes; managing budgets; setting performance targets; deciding on eligibility; and outsourcing services.

Figure 3.2. **Dashboard results for better aligning policy and programmes to local economic development**

Sub-Criteria

1.1. Flexibility in the delivery of employment and vocational training policies

1.2. Capacities within employment and VET sectors

1.3. Policy co-ordination, policy integration and co-operation with other sectors

1.4. Evidence based policy making

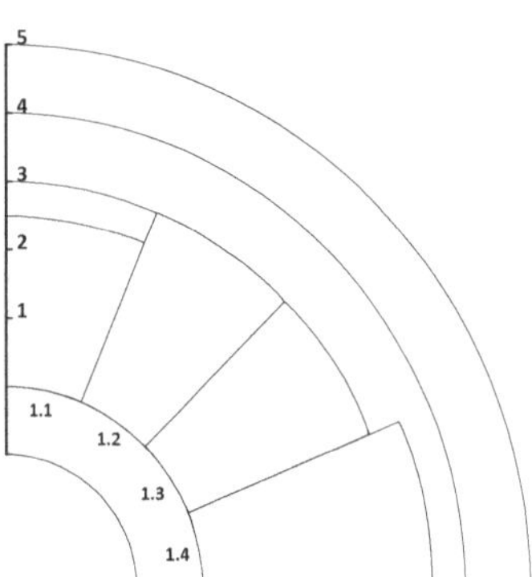

In Israel, the Public Employment Service (PES) has traditionally had to fight a poor public image relating to inefficiency in delivering labour market information and job placement assistance. Currently, much of its role is confined to determining eligibility for unemployment benefits. As such, it is not considered an agency with a strong strategic capacity for leading new labour market programmes.

Over the period from 2005-2010, the national welfare to work programme was operated independent of the PES in an attempt to generate competition and induce private sector manpower and placement agencies. This only further contributed to negative perceptions of the public employment service. A reconstituted welfare to work programmes is due to begin in 2015 and will to operate through the public employment service.

Generally, local offices of the public employment service have low flexibility in the implementation of employment and skills policies. The voucher system does allow them some flexibility in catering vocational assessment and training to the needs of workers and employers but very little local discretion with respect to budgeting and eligibility criteria which are all determined nationally.

In terms of performance management, there are no nationally-set standards or targets. Some offices report placement of 120-150 workers per year as an indicator of activities while others use duration in a job (90 days) rather than placements. In all cases, due to the volume of cases, no systematic monitoring takes place. The previous welfare to work programme linked outcomes to resources creating an incentive for the cancellation of welfare payments. However within that programme, success was equated with placement with no attention to the quality of job or time spent in employment.

As discussed previously, Employment Orientation Centres (EOCs) have been established as separate centres from the mandatory public employment service and are designed to provide one-stop services to Arab-Israeli job seekers. Participation in EOC services is voluntary and the centres are given more flexibility in the implementation of employment and skills policies. They take a 'surgical' approach to both vocational training and assessing employer's needs by targeting unskilled Arab-Israeli job seekers using a more proactive approach. The centres can chose across a suite of training courses offered by the Manpower Training and Development Bureau. In addition they can initiate their own courses or leverage the voucher system to match job seekers with commercially operated courses.

In terms of budget flexibility, they have discretion in spending across a pool of activities with the aim of matching the needs of local employers with the employment aspirations of Arab-Israeli job seekers. At the local level, the centres are expected to employ a bottom-up approach to labour market matching as well as encouraging the creation of a professional approach to employment creation within the Arab sector.

Capacities within employment and VET sectors

All local offices of the public employment service in the case study areas reported underfunding and chronic heavy caseloads during interviews undertaken for this study. For example, the Shefaram office handles 6 000 cases annually with 6 employees (e.g. a staff to job seeker ratio of 1:1000). The Nazeret Illit office handles 3000 files with 4 workers and the Haifa office has 13 employees handling a caseload of 9 000 individuals annually. Previous OECD work in Israel found that caseload to staff ratios in the public employment service were very high by OECD standards (OECD, 2013).

Figure 3.3 shows the results from an OECD questionnaire, which asked whether local public employment service offices have sufficient capacity to deliver on their organisational mandates. One can see that almost 40% of offices indicated that human resources (e.g. the number of staff) are insufficient. Furthermore, over 30% indicated that financial resources are insufficient for delivering their required objectives whereas the skills levels and local labour market knowledge of staff was perceived to be more sufficient.

Figure 3.3 **Capacity of local public employment service offices to deliver their objectives**

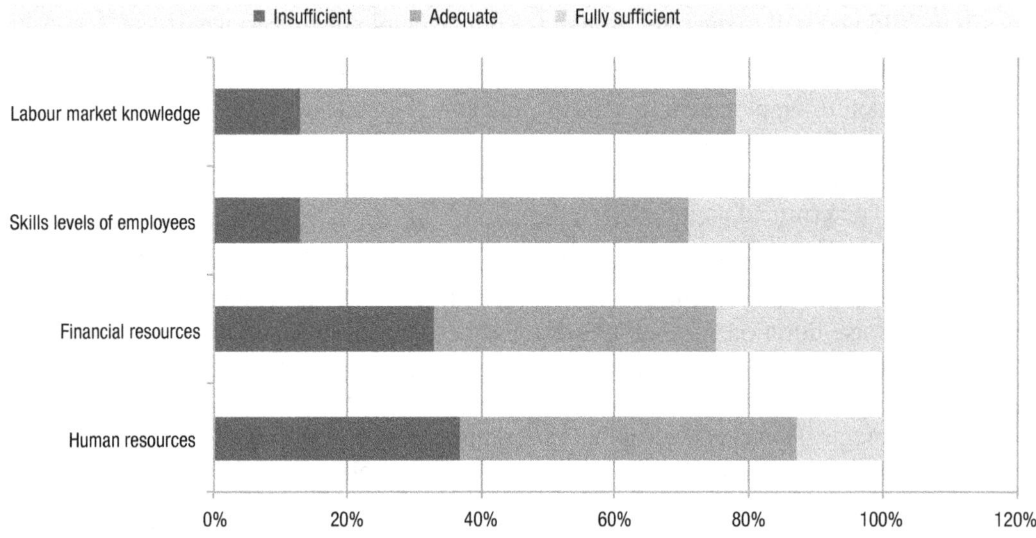

Within the Vocational Education and Training (VET) sector, there are two pathways in Israel. One is vocational education delivered through the high school system while the other is VET delivered via post compulsory education. With respect to the latter, local stakeholders report chronic underfunding over the last 10 years, which has negative implications for successful training opportunities, leading to good job opportunities among the Arab labour force.

The dominant emphasis in Israel is on the higher education (HE) track to employment. There is concern that the vocational education and training system does not have the same level of capacity. While the Arab-Israeli population is not limited to the vocational education and training system and much effort is invested in removing barriers for them to enter the higher education system, a key issue relates to increasing choice and ensuring a better match between supply and demand. Given the low level of skills among Arab-Israelis, it would seem that insufficient capacity within the vocational education and training system is counter-productive to the government's employment goals.

Policy co-ordination, policy integration, and co-operation with other sectors

The Ministry of Economy is the most significant department in the formulation of policies and programmes for employment, vocational training and economic development. This ostensibly should point to some level of linkage between activities and co-ordination between stakeholders at the national and local level. Much of the policy and programme planning is mostly top-down, which generates internal frictions at the management level between public employment services and employment orientation centres.

Figure 3.4 shows the results from the OECD questionnaire to public employment service offices on the types of organisations with whom they regularly undertake collaboration. One see that that there appears to be a high level of collaboration with private sector job placement agencies as well as employers and local authorities (92% reporting that they regularly collaborate). However, regular collaboration with colleges and training institutions was noted by 75% of offices who responded to the questionnaire. Only 58% of offices reported regular collaboration with public organisations serving minorities, and 46% reported regular collaboration with economic development offices.

Figure 3.4 **Which organisations does the public employment service collaborate with at the local level?**

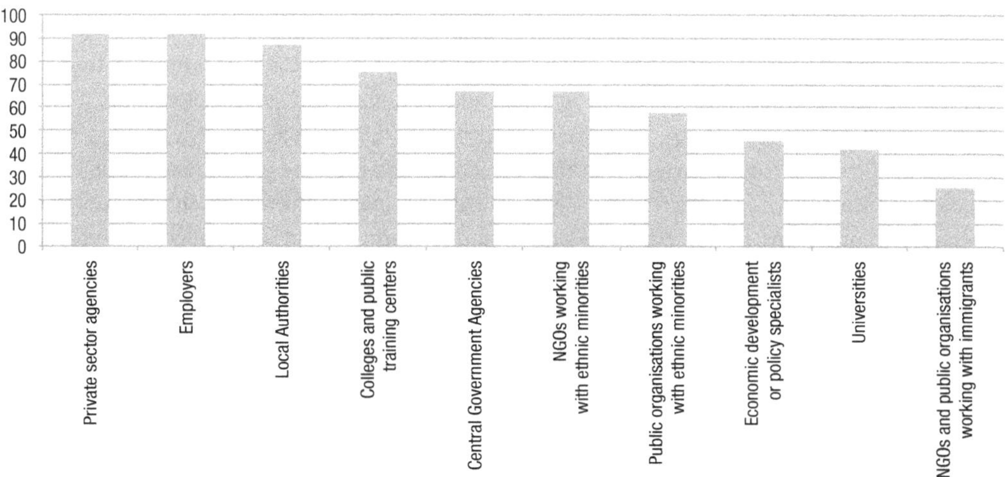

At the local level, while there appears to be some outreach by public employment service offices, in general, there are ad-hoc linkages and coordination on the basis of informal channels of communication between employers and organisations offering training and preparation as well as between central government agencies operating locally, such as the public employment service, the employment orientation centres, and vocational training organisations. Local policy coordination and integration is generally weak as many local bodies are focused on services delivery functions. No strategic local strategies or bodies exist, which define employment and skills objective for their local or regional area.

At the national level, the Authority for Economic Development of the Arab (AEDA), Druze and Circassian Sectors, established by the Prime Minister's Office in 2007, attempts to integrate and coordinate policy for employment and economic development of the Arab-Israeli population. It has a mandate to bring all the relevant agencies together as an integrated coordinating, monitoring and planning body. Presently, the AEDA has budget of over 2 billion NIS and is engaged in a multi-sectoral five-year development plan for the economic development of the Arab community. An example of a bottom-up effort at promoting local governance and policy co-ordination across local authorities is the INJAZ initiative for Professional Arab Local Governance (see Box 3.1).

A further example of potential voluntary (non-statutory) co-ordination bringing together local skills, employment and economic development efforts are the Employment Orientation Centres. As local community based initiatives, they operate local forums for employment and economic development. This serves as the arena for central government agencies, the local public employment services offices, local government departments and service providers, local business interests, local small business development centres, local training and academic institutions to brainstorm and co-operate.

Box 3.1 **INJAZ Centre for the professionalization of Arab local government**

INJAZ is an NGO located in Nazareth that serves as a lobby for greater professionalism within Arab local government. This organisation was founded in 2008 and its mandate is focused on improving the quality of local governance and policy implementation between Arab local authorities.

Traditionally, local government in Arab society has been weak, lacking the tradition of public bureaucracy that provides services and accountability to its electorate. INJAZ offers Arab language training, information and networking for elected officials and public servants allowing them to navigate central government and promote local economic and fiscal independence. INJAZ is also a resource centre that disseminates information about government assistance, procurement and contracts and provides seminars and workshops to keep local government professionals aware of the latest developments in the spheres of legislation and judicial information. INJAZ attempts to enhance local governance by coordinating between heads of cities and local councils, providing information and assisting in the interaction with national government.

This is of particular significance as despite the inherent weaknesses and inefficiencies, local authorities are still the main representative arena for the Arab population. INJAZ has the potential to act as a regional strategic body given its local orientation.

Evidence based policy making

Standard labour force data is available from the Labour Force Surveys conducted by the Central Bureau of Statistics. While there are issues with these surveys relating to sample representativeness for small localities, this is still a useful data source that is under-utilised at the local level. Reporting from the local level to the national level exists in a variety of formats. For example, technological and vocational training outputs are monitored by the Manpower Training and Development Bureau and the Department of Education.

Additionally, local employment services offices report to the national level with respect to the volume of caseload files, and job placements. The Employment Orientation Centres will follow and monitor each participant over a 3 year period. This data is generally available on-line and shared across the relevant government agencies. However, it is unclear the extent to which all the relevant data is in fact collated and analysed as well as the extent to which it is used for evaluation purposes.

In terms of national evaluation and monitoring of specific programmes over time, there appears to be a limited number of good examples. The EOC's are to undergo a national evaluation due to report in 2017. While a comprehensive number of programmes have been introduced in recent years, it is hard to get any sense of how efficient they are or even their success (output) rates. No accepted evaluation criteria are used or published (e.g. cost per job, and/or return per input of investment). Pilot programmes are often monitored over the short term especially by NGOs such as JDC-TEVET. Their reports are available but the extent to which they influence policy making is limited. Policy making can be influenced by non-government organisations and extra-parliamentary interest groups (witness the case of the Welfare to Work programme) but this is due to political pressure rather than systematic and robust evidence-based analysis.

Theme 2: Adding value through skills

Figure 3.5 **Dashboard results for adding value through skills**

Sub-Criteria

1.1. Flexible training open to all in a broad range of sectors
1.2. Working with employers on training
1.3. Matching people to jobs and facilitating progression
1.4. Joined up approaches to skills

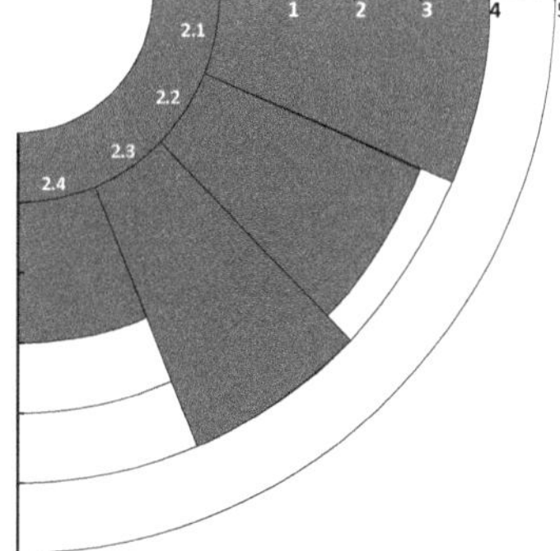

Flexible training open to all in a broad range of sectors

Nationally, about 8 000 unemployed people representing about 1.7% of the total unemployed population participate in vocational training. While this is a low by OECD standards, attempts are made to tailor the diverse training needs of those seeking training to the demands of the market. Vocational training starting at the school level (vocational classes) or delivered via dedicated training institutions at the post–high school level, offer a wide range of professional skills. An example is the Tamra vocational centre funded by the Manpower Training and Development Bureau. This centre offers training in 10 major sectors such as construction, auto mechanics, metal work, carpentry, fashion, child care, administration and 31 professions. All these lead to nationally recognised certifications. This centre has provided over 500 courses over the last 18 years and requires a minimum of 18 participants to open a course.

Softer skills such as writing CV's, preparing for interviews, organisational and presentation skills, basic Hebrew and English, professional and psychological counselling, and basic computer orientation are provided by the Employment Orientation Centres, public employment services and various non-government organisations and run from 3-12 months in length. Subsidised funding for up to 90% of a course (to a threshold level of 9 000 NIS) is available from the Ministry of Economy. For those choosing courses run by recognised private sector training centres, the same level of funding is available via the voucher system under the aegis of the public employment service. In 2011, around 1 500 vouchers were issued to job seekers, which fell short of the government target of 20% of vocational training for adults being implemented by the voucher system. Outcomes of the voucher system appear to be strong as 74% of those who participated were employed five months after completion, with 47% of them working in an occupation for which they were trained, 22% were unemployed, and 5% were outside of the labour market (MOITAL, 2012).

The public employment service also offers soft skill workshops related to finding work, personal coaching for entry to the labour market and labour market rehabilitation workshops for those seeking to re-enter after a long period of non-participation. Figure 3.6 shows the results from the OECD questionnaire distributed to local public employment service offices, which asked for the types of training interventions that are generally undertaken with minority groups. Vocational training and coaching for job interviews are a common practice whereas only 37% of offices responded that delivering or referring unemployed individuals to basic skills training is a common intervention. Considering that skill levels are lower among Arab-Israelis, this is an area of activity, which warrants further attention.

Within the case study areas, a large selection of heterogeneous target groups exist with very different training needs. Even within sub populations, variations exist therefore, this may explain why there is no 'one size fits all' framework for training. It may also explain the range of different organisations active in this area. Box 3.2 provides an example of a local initiative dedicated to providing training to long-term unemployed individuals.

There is one vocational education and technological training college that exists in Israel, which is targeted to the Arab population (the Tamra Technological Center). It offers training in 19 programmes and serves 55 Arab, Druze and Bedouin communities in the north of the country (with total population of 700,000). Additionally, there is a private Arab academic college in Israel - the Nazareth Academic Institute (NAI) - an organisation with about 150 students and two degree tracks in chemistry and media studies.

Vocational training operated by the private sector is incorporated into national policy via the voucher system. There is also some vocational training that is operated by NGOs, which is targeted to specific groups. For example, the Beatzmi NGO focuses on empowering women with low education and encouraging their entry to the workforce. The *Tzofen* NGO concentrates on encouraging Arabs to work in high tech and the the *Kav Mashveh* NGO on preparing Arab workers for the labour market.

Figure 3.6 **Types of activities that are delivered, funded, or referred by the public employment service to people from minorities**

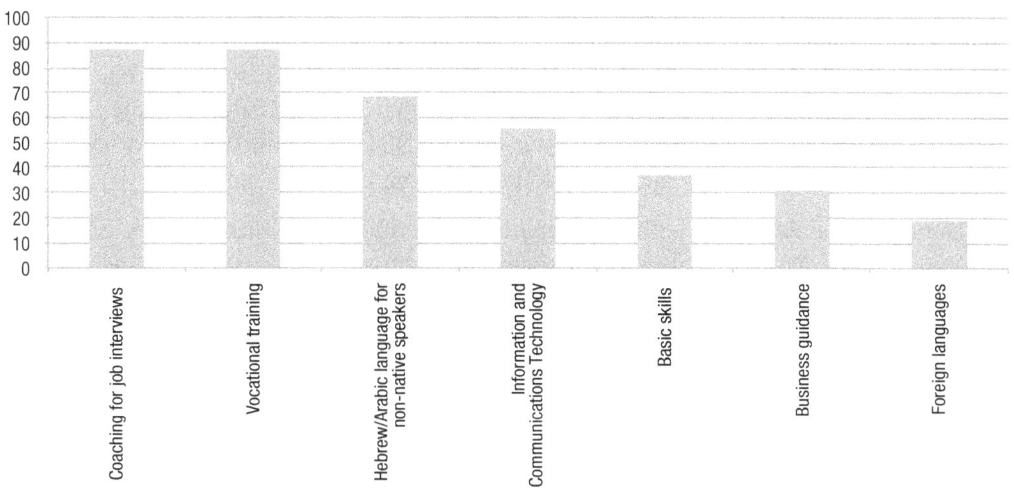

Box 3.2. Targeting training to the long-term unemployed and Arab-Israelis

Be-Atzmi is a public-private non-profit partnership operating since 1995, which is dedicated to assisting long term and chronically unemployed integrate into the workforce. It runs seven employment programmes in a variety of locations including Nazareth and Shefaram. Programmes are catered to target sub populations such as ultra-orthodox, single parents Arabs and new immigrants.

A central programme offered for the Arab population is Masar ('Path' in Arabic) which is targeted at Arab women with less than 12 years education who are looking to move into the labour market. The programme provides tailored mentoring service for candidates seeking entry to the labour market. They are provided with the soft skills and basic computer literacy training to ease the transition from home to work but the programme does not provide job placement support.

The programme assists less the 120 women each year in six Arab communities nationally. Be'atzmi ('On My Own' in Hebrew) is the implementing organisation for the Eshet Hayil/ Rivadiya ('Women of Valor' in Hebrew/Arabic) women's employment initiative programme run by the Ministry of Welfare. This programme which has similar aims to Masar, was initiated by the JDC-Tevet in the 1990s for Ethiopian women and has been extended to include Arab women in 13 communities.

Working with employers on training

Most employer involvement in training is through vocational programmes operated by the Manpower Training and Development Bureau. On the job training (OJT) is available, where a new worker is assigned an in-house mentor in the workplace for up to 12 months. The employer is reimbursed for cost of training, receives a subsidy for the worker and must commit to employing the trainee. The worker does not receive an official accreditation for participation. Another option is in-house training, where employers propose an in-house course, recruit the potential candidates and must commit to employing 65% of those graduating. Trainees receive official accreditation. There are difficulties in increasing the popularity of working with employers on training, which stems from a reluctance of employers to commit to hiring graduates, the risk that more mobile graduates will not stay long enough to realise a return on their training and the administration of getting an in-house training programme approved (King and Eyal, 2012).

There is some flexibility within the training system to ensure that it can be adapted to employer's needs. A variety of ways for partnering with employers is offered and attempts are made to provide individual responses in terms of training needs. Engagement with other stakeholders such as NGOs is encouraged and co-operation in funding and sharing training facilities is common. However much of this is ad hoc and not institutionalised in nature. Similarly, the level of employer involvement in training is still limited. 20% of the government training budget is meant to be utilised for on the job training. It is hard to gauge the share of payroll invested by employers in training because this data is not collected but the impression from case study interviews undertaken for this study is that it is low.

The public employment service is less proactive in working with employers on training. Traditionally, VET has been perceived as a mechanism for easing welfare recipients into the labour force and has been linked to eligibility for the income benefits administered by the public employment service. Over time, this eligibility has been cut back and a more targeted approach to specific population groups has been adopted. Occasionally, a local public employment service office might conduct outreach to local employers for example by organising an employment fair but in general this is not a common activity.

Working with SMEs on skills development activities is provided by the Small Business Authority and delivered locally by the Small Business Development Centres (SBDCs). The SBDCs engage in entrepreneurial training, assistance in business plan preparation and grants for vocational training. About 350 courses of this kind are conducted annually. In 2010, 80 courses were organised in the Arab sector catering for 1600 participants (approximately two thirds of these in the North of Israel).

Matching people to jobs and facilitating progression

Much effort is expended by all stakeholders in the area of job placement support. To this end, effort is put into the 'surgical' training and guidance of job seekers into particular labour market openings. However, there is little systematic follow-through, post placement. This is either because of a lack of resources or a general reticence towards labour market tracking. Consequently, it is not known whether economic welfare rises once placed in work, whether the placement has an long-term employment horizon and prospects for labour market mobility and/or the general quality of the job.

This leads to an inordinate emphasis on 'counting jobs' as a metric of success and generating 'flexibility' amongst populations in the labour market. Removal of barriers is considered a goal in itself with the resultant focus on provision of transportation, preparation of industrial zones in small places where they have little chance of survival. There is an absence of attention to job quality, career pathways, mobility opportunities and pay levels.

Joined up approaches to skills

Given the fact that most of the stakeholders operating at the local level are local service delivery offices for national government, their over-arching priority is the delivery of national policy. Local stakeholders such as local authorities have a more local view to retaining local talent and attracting investment. Practically however, there are very few tools at their disposal. Most sub districts such as the study areas highlighted are not self-contained labour markets and as such it is difficult to ensure that 'local' jobs go to local people. Furthermore, as mentioned earlier, for local authorities, local economic development is not about jobs but about property tax and increasing local fiscal autonomy. Despite the plethora of stakeholders operating in the study area, it is hard to point to a joined up approach to skills.

Theme 3: Targeting policy to local employment sectors and investing in quality jobs

Figure 3.7 **Dashboard results for targeting policy to local employment sectors and investing in quality jobs**

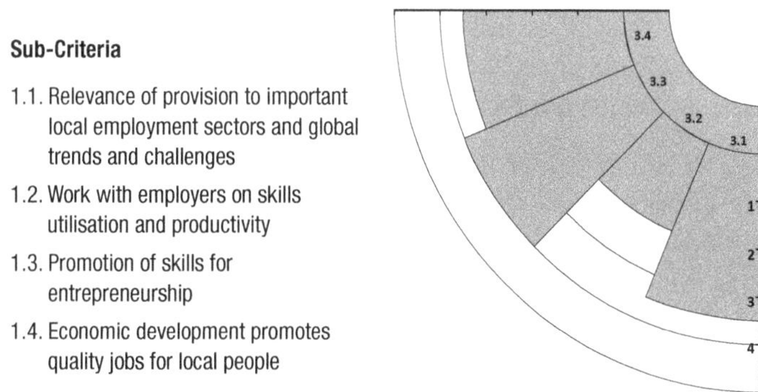

Relevance of provision to important local employment sectors and global trends and challenges

Informal connections between local stakeholders leads to targeting in as much as stakeholders working on the supply side (e.g. the public employment service, employment orientation centres, and NGOs) attempt to channel their efforts to the needs of local employers. In this respect, local employers can be said to drive the local skills agenda. However this activity is generally on the basis of personal contacts and local knowledge. It is not coordinated in any formal way and there is no single authority charged with identifying local needs or mapping local comparative advantage.

There is an awareness of structural trends in the Israeli economy (e.g. the shift to high tech, the demand for labour intensive personal services) and their detrimental impact over the short term on weaker sectors of the labour market. Attempts exist to provide the soft skills for navigating the demands of the modern labour market. One such area is the growing awareness within the Arab sector of the need to provide health care services for senior citizens. This breaks with the tradition of caring for the elderly within the nuclear family but generates a previously un-met demand and provides employment opportunities for workers at a skill level for which adequate supply exists in the case study areas.

Within the case study areas, there are various initiatives that match worker training programmes to local employment sectors. For example, the Tamra vocational training centre offers vocational and technician training in those skills areas that serve the heavy industries located in the Haifa and Acre areas such as welding and CNC operators. The Employment Orientation Centres operating in the case study areas have a pilot programme incorporating Arab engineers in the Haifa high tech and IT cluster, in co-operation with the Tsofen NGO and the JDC-TEVET.

Work with employers on skills utilisation and productivity

The public sector can help to build better quality jobs by working with employers on issues of skills utilisation and productivity. Skills utilisation approaches involve looking at how companies are using the existing skills base of employees within their company and adjusting production processes to stimulate productivity. It can also involve workplace training programmes for employees to further develop their skills contributing to incremental innovation.

This study did not find a strong awareness at the local level about the role that public policy can play in ensuring employers better utilise the skills of their workforce. In general, job quality and working conditions and remuneration are not treated as local issues. Labour unions are involved in these areas in terms of negotiating national standards and wage bargaining agreements, which are then applied locally.

Given the skills structure and occupational distribution of the Arab-Israeli labour force, those employed in industrial sectors are likely to have their labour conditions monitored by the relevant unions. In contrast, those working in the service areas are in a much more precarious position. Many of them are on short term contracts, employed by manpower companies that pay close to minimum wages and offer very little in terms of social benefits and pensions.

Promotion of skills for entrepreneurship

Training for entrepreneurship is delivered via the national network of 23 small business centres. In the case study areas, three centres exist in Haifa, Nazareth and Nazeret Illit. Each Small Business Development Centre (SBDC) is independent with different sources of funding. For example, the Haifa SBDC is supported by the Ministry of Economy, the Haifa municipality and the Jewish Federation of Boston. All however offer the same mix of core training for entrepreneurship (see Box 3.3).

VET activity places less emphasis on entrepreneurship as a core skill although training is offered in business management but less in finance, writing business plans and market surveys. Finally, local educational institutes (regional colleges and universities) will offer courses in entrepreneurial training but rarely degree programmes in entrepreneurship.

Box 3.3 **Nazareth Small Business Development Centre (MATI)**

MATI is one of a national network of 23 Small Business Development Centers (SBDCs). The Nazareth centre was established in 2008 and employs 17 workers. It operates on the basis of joint funding from the MOE, MDGN, the local authority and chamber of commerce and overseas NGOs. Like all SBDCs, it provides the usual suite of subsidised assistance for small entrepreneurs looking to start a business including initial counselling, feasibility, business and financial planning and a revolving loan fund.

Beyond the start-up stage, small businesses can get individualised or group assistance with marketing and sales, human resource management, production management and exporting. The Nazareth SBDC also caters to unique local niches. To that end, it operates a tourism incubator and specialised courses to encourage the commercialisation of local skills such as ethnic needlework. It also targets population groups looking to participate in the labour market such as Arab female, first-time entrants offering basic soft skills and business counselling. In a given year, the SBDC will run approximately 50 programmes with 15 participants in each.

Economic development promotes quality jobs for local people

When large scale inward investment is attracted (for example the Intel fabrication plant in Kiryat Gat in the south of Israel) it is not expected that the local labour force would supply the new demand. Large scale investment very quickly absorbs the limited skill supply offered locally and then starts to mop up talent from other regions. A similar phenomenon is noted with respect to the Amdocs high tech plant in Nazareth that feels that it is exhausting local high skilled labour supply. As Israel is a small and compact country, skill needs can be met from other areas as long as the place generating demand is within the commuting orbit of a major pool of skilled labour. There is a strong emphasis on generating demand by attracting investment or establishing investment funds (see Box 3.5) needs to ensure that there is an appropriate supply-side capacity in terms of human capital.

Local stakeholders such as local authorities and non-government organisations are generally not consulted in the negotiations with inward investors. These are conducted at the national (central government) level and generally by-pass local authorities. This marginalisation is even more acute in the case of Arab local authorities which are viewed as unprofessional and lacking in management skills necessary to promote economic development. Large scale investment (especially foreign investment) is attracted to Israel, rather than to particular locales within the country. Local authorities are more focused on providing tax breaks, subsidised rents and ensuring good infrastructure. Furthermore, local job creation is not a criterion in public procurement bids or construction tenders.

Aside from employment and training courses, assistance to disadvantaged groups can also relate to microfinance and small business capitalisation. For example, dedicated loan funds and microfinance lending circles have been set up for assisting Ethiopian women and Arab women (see Box 3.4).

Box 3.4 **The Al Bawader investment fund**

The Koret Foundation Israel Economic Development Fund (KIEDF) is a US-funded NGO with a mission of expanding the private sector in Israel. If focuses primarily on supporting small business via a series of loan funds, micro-finance programmes and targeting initiatives including a dedicated Israeli-Arab Loan Fund and a microfinance fund for Arab women. KIEDF leverages funds from commercial banks and partners with government agencies including the Authority for the Economic Development of the Arab Sector, the Small Business Authority and the Ministry of Economy.

It has pioneered microfinance as a tool for the economic empowerment of women in different ethnic communities (Ethiopian, Bedouin and Arab). The SAW ('Together' in Arabic) Microfinance Programme provides direct seed loans (between $1-5,000). It operates reciprocal group solidarity lending circles as pioneered by the Grameen Bank and is the only source of non-bank microfinance in Israel. The SAW programme was initially started for the Bedouin community but has subsequently expanded to include Arab women within the study area. Half of the operating costs and capitalisation of the programme now comes from the AEDA.

Theme 4: Being inclusive

Figure 3.8 **Dashboard results for being inclusive**

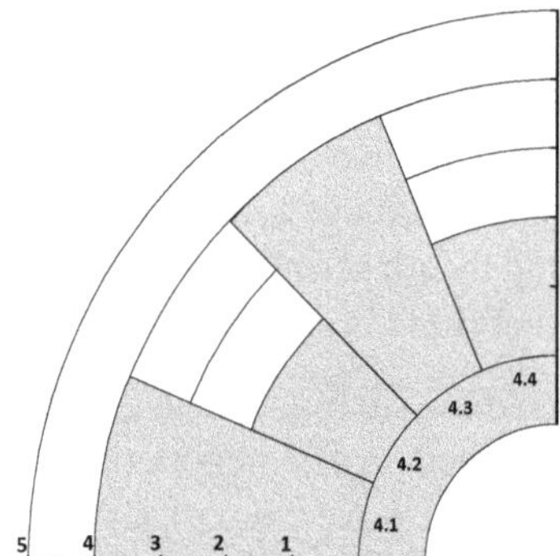

Employment and training programmes are geared to local 'at-risk' groups

A strong emphasis is placed on targeting the needs of employment and skills programmes to the needs of 'at risk' groups. Both the public employment service and the Manpower Training and Development Bureau channel their services (e.g. employment counselling and vocational training) to the needs of individual population groups. There are also a range of non-government organisations operating a number of dedicated programmes with a mandate to assist specific disadvantaged populations, including Arab-Israeli, Ethiopian immigrants, youth drop-outs, Arab-Israeli women, and single parent families.

Providing programmes to 'at risk' populations is also within the jurisdiction of the Ministry of Welfare. Traditionally, this government agency has dealt with improving the employment chances of the disabled. Over the years however, it has extended its employment mandate to include other at-risk populations including victims of violence, substance abusers, Ethiopian immigrants, kids at risk and people from dysfunctional families. The Ministry of Welfare has an employment administration that deals with increasing the participation of these groups through a variety of small scale initiatives. The ministry operates over 50 programmes with over 30,000 participants – about 50% of which are those with disabilities. Amongst these initiatives is the *Eshet Hayil* programme operated with the JDC-TEVET and the Abraham Fund to encourage the entry of Ethiopian women into the labour market (see Box 3.5).

This model was extended to Arab women under the '*Ryadiah*' programme and in 2011 had 1400 participants – of whom, 630 were Arabs. The MOW offers other employment-focused services such as the Occupational Social Worker (OSW) who assists families with long histories of unemployment or under-employment. Each OSW services up to 50 families and the model has been adopted in 20 small towns. Additionally, the MOW runs the '*Maavarim*' programme (alternatively known as the Employment Oriented Regional Authority). This attempts to bring together key employment stakeholders and co-ordinate employment activity in rural communities. It operates in 7 places (including 2 localities in the study areas) offering services to 1500 participants.

Figure 3.9 shows the results from the OECD questionnaire about the general activities of the public employment service in working with employers on activities related to minority groups. From the responses received, all offices conduct outreach with employers to see what job opportunities are available for minority groups. Furthermore, one can also see that there is a strong focus on placing minorities into vacant positions (88% responded that they undertake this type of activity).

Figure 3.9 **Types of work undertaken by the public employment service with employers regarding minority groups**

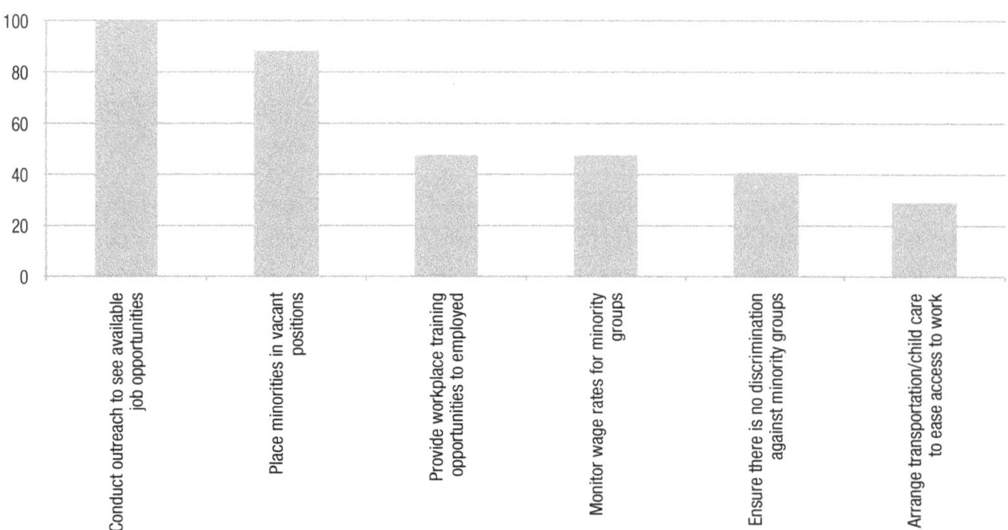

By default, programmes by the Ministry of Welfare are geared towards pockets of deprivation. In contrast, other stakeholders dealing with at risk populations (e.g. the public employment service and Manpower Training and Development Bureau) are invariably 'people' rather than 'place' based.

Box 3.5 **The Abraham Fund**

The Abraham Fund is a non-governmantal organsiation with a traditional interest in promoting Jewish-Arab coexistence through philanthropic projects in the areas of education and culture. Over time, its focus has shifted to project incubation and developing working coexistence models in the areas of public policy and institutional reform with a view to closing gaps between Arab and Jewish societies.

In the areas of employment and skills, the Abraham Fund operates the Sharikay Haya ('Life Partner' in Arabic) initiative which involves training placement and support for Arab female first time entrants in the labour market. Modelled on the JDC-Tevet Eshet Hayil/Rivadiya programme, this initiative provides over 300 hours of training to each participant and the Sharikat Haya women group model has been included in the national expansion of the Eshet Hayil/Rivadiya programme funded by the Ministries of Welfare and Economy.

Investment funds have also been set-up focused on the Arab-Israeli sector. For example, through a joint venture between the AEDA and the private sector established in 2009 as a result of a government tender, the AEDA committed 80 million NIS to match funding from partnerships which encourage private sector investment within the manufacturing, ICT and high tech sectors. As a consequence, the Pitango venture capital company established the Al Bawader ('the bud' in Arabic) investment fund and raised 100 million NIS from private investors. To date, the company has invested in 7 software and internet start-ups providing the usual business monitoring and counseling services offered by venture capital companies. Ultimately the fund expects to have a portfolio of 15 companies that it will assist through the process of raising capital, marketing and entering export markets.

Childcare and family friendly policies to support women's participation in employment

Access to child care is considered a key issue towards increasing Arab female labour market participation. Consequently, in recent years, more public support has been given to child care policies and programmes, which aim to increase the supply of labour. Adding funding for child care services to total active labour market policy spending raises the share of public support for these types of instruments from 0.2% of GDP to 0.3%.

Over the last two years, the Ministry of Economy has supported the construction of 36 new child care centres in the North of Israel doubling the availability of such facilities in the Arab sector. Each one of these centres can cater for up to 100 children up to the age of 3 and they are run by local authorities and non-governmental organisations. Fees are subsidised by the Ministry of Economy for the Arab sector. For example, the eligibility criterion for subsidy for Arab women in part-time employment is 24 weekly hours of work whereas the corresponding figure for Jewish women is 36 hours. Additionally, the Ministry of Economy regulates the price within family day care centres. These are small-scale private, child care services that comprise a child-minder and 5-6 children. They voluntarily agree to price control for 5 years and in return the government funds their adaptation to meet national standards. There are currently 1200 such child care places within this type of arrangement catering to children within the Arab sector.

Fully subsidised pre-school education is available universally in Israel and acts as a further incentive to stimulate labour market participation. As school finishes in the early afternoon, a further afternoon educational framework is also available for children aged 3-9. Subsidies for these programmes are available in all communities with a low socio-economic composition (most of the small towns in the study area) and are not subject to a minimum number of weekly working hours. These recent developments stem from recommendations of the Trajtenberg Committee in 2012.

Another barrier to labour force participation is inadequate transportation or shuttle services to places of employment and child care arrangements. In responding to the OECD questionnaire, only 29% of public employment service offices responded that they undertake these types of activity (see Figure 3.9 above).

The Ministry of Economy along with the Ministry of Transportation (MOT) have outlined work programmes for upgrading accessibility between Arab villages and centres of employment. These include road investment, extending public transportation lines and operating shuttle/worker transportation services to employment centres at subsidised rates. For example, the recent extension of public bus transport lines to the Druze towns of Daliat El Carmel and Ussafiya means easies access to the employment centre at Yokneam, the Trans Israel highway and the University of Haifa. Larger scale transportation investments are also slated to have a long term impact, such as the Haifa- Bet Shean rail line (via Afula) and the light rail from Haifa to Nazareth.

Tackling youth unemployment

Stakeholders in the study areas tend to cite youth unemployment in the Arab sector as a burning labour issue quoting unemployment rates of 30-40%. Taking a broad definition of youth unemployment (18-24 years), official statistical data do not show unemployment of this magnitude. Over the last decade, Jewish youth unemployment has generally been higher than its Arab counterpart.

However due to the fact that all Jewish and Druze youth go straight to the army or national civic service after school, the share of NEET (not in Education, Employment or Training) in the Arab sector is high, especially for the 18-21 age group. Arab school-leavers lack the contacts and in-roads to employment that army/national service can offer. They enter the labour market without the informal networks available to the Jewish and Druze counterparts which gives them access to better job opportunities. Additionally completion of national/military service offers further employment benefits in terms of subsidised higher education and vocational training.

Greater participation in national civic service on the part of the Arab community might be an option to increase their access to quality jobs. Currently, less than 2 500 Arabs choose this track when completing high school – of which 90% are women. However, this is a loaded political issue that would need further reflection and analysis.

Openness to immigration

As an immigrant society, Israel is attuned to the needs of new immigrants. The Ministry of Immigrant Absorption offers a range of education and training programmes for new immigrants. All of these are national programmes which are delivered locally by regional field offices. The existence of these programmes locally is purely contingent on the residential choices of immigrants. In the study areas, the city of Haifa and the town of Nazeret Illit have been magnets for immigrants in the past. As large scale immigration tends to come in waves (less than 20,000 immigrants per year), the existence of course and retraining schemes is contingent on the size of demand.

Israel's temporary labour migration scheme continues to remain significant, representing 12% of the labour force in 2012 (BOI, 2012). Previous work conducted by the OECD on developments and progress in labour market and social policy concluded that a sharp reduction of quotas for foreign workers would be a straightforward and efficient way of raising participation (OECD, 2013a). This review also noted that the admission of foreigner workers reduces employment prospects to low-skilled Arabs especially in the construction sector and while the quota of Palestinians working in Israel has increased, wages are still low.

References

BOI – Bank of Israel (2012), *Annual Report 2011*, Bank of Israel, Jerusalem, www.bankisrael.gov.il/

Ben-David D (2012) (ed.), *State of the Nation Report, Society, Economy and Policy in Israel 2011-12*, Taub Center for Social Policy Studies, Jerusalem.

BOI (2011), *Annual Report 2011*, Bank of Israel, Jerusalem.

Brookings Institution (2012), *Global Metro Monitor 2012*, Metropolitan Policy Program, Brookings Institution, Washington DC.

Field S and Kuczera M (2012), *A Skills Beyond School Commentary on Israel*, OECD Reviews of Vocational Education and Training, Paris.

Habib J., King J., Ben Shoham A, Wolde-Tsadick A and Lasky K (2010), *Labor Market and Socio Economic Outcomes of the Arab-Israeli Population*, OECD Social Employment and Migration Working Papers No 102, OECD, Paris. DOI: http://dx.doi.org/10.1787/5kmjnrcfsskc-en

James S., Warhurst C., Tholen G and Commander J (2013), *What we know and what we need to know about graduate skills, Work, Employment and Society*, 27(6), 952-963.

King J and Eyal Y (2012), *Vocational Education and Training (VET) Background Report for Israel, prepared for OECD Project: Skills Beyond School* Submitted by The Manpower Training and Development Bureau, The Ministry of Industry, Trade and Labour.

MOITAL (2012a), *Progress Report on the Implementation of the OECD Recommendations: Labour Market and Social Policies*, Israel, Ministry of Industry, Trade and Labor, Jerusalem.

MOITAL (2012b), Employment Status of Graduates of Vocational Training in the Voucher Programme of the Employment Services, Class 4 (2010), by Alon Porat, *www.moital.gov.il/NR/rdonlyres/CAB9D1ED-D6EC-4D89-9C2B-318AA2E05B5B/0/X12310.pdf*

Musset, P., M. Kuczera and S. Field (2014), *A Skills beyond School Review of Israel*, OECD Reviews of Vocational Education and Training, OECD Publishing. DOI: *http://dx.doi.org/10.1787/9789264210769-en*

OECD (2014), *Job Creation and Local Economic Development*, OECD Publishing, Paris. DOI: *http://dx.doi.org/10.1787/9789264215009-en*

OECD (2013), *Review of Recent Developments and Progress in Labour Market and Social Policy in Israel: Slow Progress Towards a More Inclusive Society*, OECD Publishing, Paris. DOI: *http://dx.doi.org/10.1787/9789264200401-en*

OECD (2012), *Better Skills, Better Jobs, Better Lives: A Strategic Approach to Skills Policies*, OECD Publishing, Paris. DOI: *http://dx.doi.org/10.1787/9789264177338-en*

OECD (2011), Study on the Geographic Coverage of Israeli Data, OECD Statistics Directorate, OECD, Paris, *www.oecd.org/els/48442642.pdf*

OECD (2010), *OECD Reviews of Labour Market and Social Policies: Israel*, OECD Publishing, Paris. DOI: *http://dx.doi.org/10.1787/9789264079267-en*

Persky J., Felsenstein D and Carlson V (2004), *Does 'Trickle Down' Work? Economic Development Strategies and Job Chains in Local Labor Markets*, W.E .Upjohn Institute of Employment Research Kalamazoo, MI.

Yashiv, E. and N. Kasir (2013a), *Arab Women in the Israeli Labor Market: Characteristics and Policy Proposals*, Israel Economic Review, 10 (2),.1-41.

Yashiv, E. and N. Kasir (2013b), *The Labor Market for Arab Israelis: Characteristics and Policy Choices*, Department of Public Policy, Tel Aviv University, *www.tau.ac.il/~yashiv/IsraeliArabs_policy_paper.pdf*

Yashiv, E. and N. Kasir (2011), *Patterns of Labor Force Participation Among Israeli Arabs*, Israel Economic Review, 9 (1),. 53-101.

Chapter 4

Towards an action plan for jobs in Israel: Recommendations and best practices*

Stimulating job creation at the local level requires integrated actions across employment, training, and economic development portfolios. Co-ordinated place-based policies can help workers find suitable jobs, while also contributing to demand by stimulating productivity. This requires flexible policy management frameworks, information, and integrated partnerships which leverage the efforts of local stakeholders. This chapter outlines the key recommendations emerging from the OECD review of local job creation policies in Israel.

* The statistical data for Israel are supplied by and under the responsibility of the relevant Israeli authorities. The use of such data by the OECD is without prejudice to the status of the Golan Heights, East Jerusalem and Israeli settlements in the West Bank under the terms of international law.

Better aligning programmes and policies to local economic development

Recommendation: Strengthen local policy cooperation and coordination by fostering partnerships, which can effectively design and implement employment and skills strategies targeted at Arab-Israelis

This study has highlighted the strong role that is played at the national level by a number of ministries and organisations, including the Ministry of Economy and the Authority for Economic Development for the Arab, Druze, and Circassian Sectors within the Prime Minister's Office. These departments are involved in the design and implementation of a number of programmes aimed at increasing the participation of Arab-Israelis in the labour force. Locally, there a range of private and voluntary sector initiatives but the majority of programmes operate within a top-down governance arrangement.

Employment Orientation Centres have been recently introduced to provide a one-stop suite of programmes and services targeted to the Arab-Israeli population. While implementation is still in the early stages, this initiative is a welcome development to provide culturally sensitive services to the Arab-Israeli population. The Employment Orientation Centres are well placed to significantly increase participation among the Arab-Israeli population. They have more autonomy than other government services and have a flag-ship role in this area.

Lack of public transportation and access to affordable and quality child care are major issues facing many Arab-Israelis, particularly women. Therefore, Employment Orientation Centres will need to focus on how better co-ordinate these types of services so that they can effectively generate access to good employment opportunities for Arab female first time entrants, and school leavers. This co-ordination also needs to look at the cultural barriers related to leaving the village environment, entering the labour force and working in a Jewish employment culture. Removing the obstacles to labour market participation will need to be accompanied by the provision of jobs with potential career pathways and mobility prospects.

Employment Orientation Centres could serve as an anchor organisation, which coordinates the range of services that are needed to increase the labour market success of Arab-Israelis. Partnerships at the local level are a key governance tool that can be used by Employment Orientation Centres to better connect with other employment, skills, and economic development actors. Partnerships and networks are critical to join up skills efforts, minimise policy and programme duplication, and develop strategic objectives. Local and regional contexts are the settings where "coalitions of purpose" can be effectively built across the public, private and not-for-profit sectors, with local actors often building long-term relationships with each other based on proximity and exchange (OECD, 2014).

Going forward, Israel should seek to establish regional and/or local networks, which bring together relevant stakeholders within the employment, skills, and economic portfolios with local leaders, employers, and other relevant organisations. While local government is often perceived as weak and inefficient, it needs to be a partner in this process. It is important to ensure vertical dialogue between the local authorities and the central government as well as horizontal dialogue between local stakeholders.

Box 4.1 How to build successful partnerships?

A locally-based partnership is usually designed to bring together all relevant actors within a region to address a specific issue within a community and/or improve its overall economic well-being. However, bringing together all relevant actors is not an easy task as this implies having around one table not only different government institutions (usually of different levels), but also social partners, employers, NGOs, training institutions, and representatives of civil society. Whatever the reason to set up a partnership, there are certain factors to bear in mind:

- Organisational structure: To be efficient, a partnership should have recognisable and autonomous structure to help establish its identity. The structure should have stability and permanence as well as flexibility, and it is helpful if there is a certain independence from political influence. It is also important to review lines of communication to ensure that all partners are kept informed and involved. Equity should be a guiding principle in building a partnership, as should (for many partnerships) a "bottom-up" structure. Sufficient human and financial resources are also needed.
- Preparation: Preparatory work is crucial for developing a steady and effective partnership. Careful research into the context in which the partnership will be operating must be part of this phase. The strengths and weaknesses of the area should be assessed and effective measures designed. One of the most important aspects of this phase is to identify the right partners and establish clear roles for each.
- Work plan: Partnerships need to develop a long-term strategy if they are to work effectively and have a lasting effect. For area based partnerships, this strategy should include a vision for the region, focusing on the outcome to be achieved, an action plan identifying shorter-term priorities, and a co-ordinated working programme including activities and measures that will contribute to the achievement of long-term outcomes. The work programme should indicate the interests and targets of all partners and include activities and measures that will contribute to the improvement of the territory.
- Implementation: In this phase partners are in regular contact to co-ordinate implementation, to extend and supplement the working programme with new measures, and in some cases to test new approaches. Public relations activities should inform the wider public of the targets, activities and measures of the partnership.
- Monitoring: To assess a partnership's achievements, determine improvements to be made and adapt further planning, a comprehensive monitoring system should be used. A partnership should be evaluated periodically and publish reports to demonstrate the added value of its work.

Source: OECD (2014), *Job Creation and Local Economic Development*, OECD Publishing. DOI: http://dx.doi.org/10.1787/9789264215009-en

Actions to improve partnerships, such as the establishment of collective goals across local stakeholders, can be effective in bringing employers and jobs into a locality (Froy et al., 2011). Regional and local actors can play a critical role in articulating a vision of the future for the local economy and what measures are necessary to drive economic growth in an inclusive and sustainable manner. Often, partnerships are not effective if they are not afforded sufficient flexibility to influence and adapt employment and skills policies at the local level. Therefore, the government should consider the extent to which local partnerships could take more of a lead role in building community ownership in the implementation of policies targeted at the labour force participation of Arab-Israelis. One way would be to inject flexibility within the policy management framework to enable these partnerships to design locally customised strategies. For example, this could be achieved by piloting a local initiative where a small pool of funding could be provided to a local partnership that has demonstrated an ability to effectively deliver employment and skills strategies targeted to the Arab-Israeli population.

When considering whether to award greater flexibility, policy makers should ensure that the level of governance is right. It is important that local employment agencies are working at the level of homogenous travel to work areas or local labour markets. Furthermore and equally important in the Israeli context, local capacities need to also be considered when granting flexibility to local employment and training agencies. A "chicken and egg" situation often appears to exist in relation to capacities at the local level. National governments fear that local capacities are low and are reluctant to offer new responsibility and hence new resources. Therefore, national actors must take into consideration the capacity that exists at the local level.

To create strategic local thinking and to bolster local governance structures, policy makers in Israel could look at the governance structure of local Workforce Investment Boards (WIBs) in the United States. Local WIBs are governed by a board comprised of business and civic leaders and to a lesser extent representatives of social service organisations, educational agencies and labour groups (OECD, 2014b). The federal legislation, which established the local WIBs requires that at least 51% of the board members to be business leaders so that the needs of businesses are readily taken into account in designing and delivering employment services. Adapting this model within the Israeli context would foster greater dialogue between national and local stakeholders and also across organisations at the local level. In other OECD countries, other governance structures have been established to better connect actors at the local level.

For example, in Ontario, Canada there are 25 Workforce Planning Boards who conduct localised labour market research and actively engage organisations and community partners. Every local workforce planning board publishes detailed reports about its local labour market challenges and prospects. While they do not receive funding to introduce local initiatives, they identify and articulate potential local workforce development solutions for their communities to the provincial and federal level and serve a coordinating and networking function among the stakeholders involved.

Recommendation: Build effective monitoring and evaluation systems at the local level to understand what works in effectively removing labour market barriers and stimulating job creation and economic development opportunities

To effectively raise the labour force participation of Arab-Israelis, it will be critical to establish a strong evaluation culture. This can only be done if a monitoring and evaluation process is developed based on suitable local data and indicators. While there is a lot of local employment and economic development activity, it is unclear how effective programmes are due to a weak number of evaluations that are undertaken. The ability for local actors and partnerships to identify and respond to the barriers that some people face to getting into employment is shaped by the availability of adequate, timely local level data. Local data can also stimulate effective local partnerships, acting as a catalyst to action (Froy and Giguère, 2010).

In Israel, there should be a greater focus on evaluating policies and programmes, and feeding findings from robust evaluations into the policy development cycle so that activities and their impacts can be continuously improved. There is a need for the systematic monitoring of programme outcomes; the generation of evaluation criteria and their application to the programmes; the generation of data on post work placement; and local labour market intelligence which is relevant to the spatial units being analysed. Monitoring, evaluation and ex post placement success all need to be taken into account when trying to measure the success of a programme.

In relation to the Employment Orientation Centres, it will be important to understand what types of jobs they are creating for Arab-Israelis, as well as other outcomes, such as how long people remain employed after receiving services or whether they continue onto training to build their skills for good local job opportunities. Without systematic monitoring and evaluation metrics in Israel, none of these important policy considerations can be can be answered.

In other OECD countries, too often monitoring and evaluation appears to be overlooked and underfunded, partly due to the difficulties of conducting robust evaluations at the local level, and establishing realistic control groups and counterfactuals. National governments can help here by conducting their own evaluations at a larger scale, piloting projects in some areas and then helping to disseminate what works. At the national level there is a need for a National Employment Authority for formulating and implementing labour market policy, monitoring the labour market, and regulating the supply side (skills training, on-going training). The Ministry of Economy is the natural candidate to undertake these types of activists.

Box 4.2 The What Works Centre in the United Kingdom

A "What Works Centre" has been established by the government of the United Kingdom to promote evidence-based policy making and evaluation at the local level. Upon its inception in 2013, it has conducted a review of over 1000 policy evaluations, evidence reviews and meta-analyses from the UK and other OECD countries. This exercise has produced the following findings:

- Many evaluations are not sufficiently robust – only 71 of the above evaluations met the required standards.
- Training has a positive impact on participant's employment and earnings in more than half of the evaluations reviewed.
- In-firm/on-the-job training programmes outperform classroom based training programmes. Employer co-design and activities that closely mirror actual jobs appear to be key design elements
- The state of the economy is not a major factor in the performance of training programmes. Programme design features appear to be more important in influencing the success of the programmes examined than macroeconomic factors.

Source: What Works Centre for Local Economic Growth (2014). "Evidence Review: Employment Training", *www.whatworksgrowth.org*.

Adding value through skills

Recommendation: Increase the overall level of skills of the Arab-Israeli population through stronger skills development opportunities

This study has highlighted a wide variety of skills development programmes that are available at the local level. However, there is a much stronger emphasis on higher education within Israel with a lower status attached to the vocational education and training system. Indeed, there has been a significant decline in funding for vocational education since 2002 and changes in the unemployment benefits legislation, meaning that a small number of unemployed individuals participate in vocational training (OECD, 2010). This is a critical issue with regard to the Arab-Israeli population who have a lower level of skills relative the Jewish population. It is necessary to raise the overall status of the vocational education system and ensure that it is providing quality skills development opportunities that link with a qualifications framework which is fully recognised by employers.

Skills are a key route out of poverty and play a critical role in equipping individuals for long-term success. In Israel, there is a need to ensure that vocational education and training are a central part of the skills agenda. Recent OECD research has emphasised the potential role that vocational training can provide with regard to the demand for technical and professional skills (Kis and Park, 2012). In order to ensure that Israel does not miss-out on the economic benefits that a strong skills system can deliver, there needs to be greater emphasis on ensuring people participate in training and learning opportunities at every stage throughout their careers. Putting in place the appropriate incentives for both individuals and firms to support skills development is one way participation can be increased.

With respect to the Arab workforce, the issue seems to be one of finding the appropriate balance between building generic and more occupationally specific skills. In many cases, Arab-Israelis require strong employability skills, such as basic literacy and numeracy training whereas it is also important they have good access to intermediate and higher-skills development opportunities, which can be attained through the vocational education and training system. Results from the OECD questionnaire indicated a small proportion of public employment services offices generally refer unemployed individuals to basic skills and literacy training. For the Employment Orientation Centres that are targeted to the Arab-Israeli population, it will be important that these centres equip individuals with the basic skills necessary for labour market success as a first step before focusing on placing them into a job. This study has highlighted the surgical approach that tends to be taken by the EOCs in their early stages with a strong focus on job placement services. In many cases, individuals need appropriate skills training opportunities before they are able to successfully retain employment over the long-term.

Recommendation: Create more apprenticeship and on the job training opportunities for Arab-Israelis

In many OECD countries, there has been increasing interest in apprenticeships both as a route into employment and also in raising the skill levels of the workforce. Apprenticeship systems provide a number of career pathways for youth to develop skills and attachment to the labour market. Apprenticeships and other work-based training programmes are a well-tested mechanism for generating workplace opportunities, generating local linkages, and easing the school-work transitions. Apprenticeships and work-based training opportunities are under-valued and under-utilised in Israel with 30% of upper secondary students enrolled in technological or vocational paths, but only 4% receiving training with employers during their studies (OECD, 2013; OECD, 2014).

There are a number of benefits from developing a strong work-based learning system, including providing students with strong practical on the job learning experiences and developing stronger labour force attachment. For employers, apprenticeships can strengthen their engagement and involvement with the vocational education and training system and lead to increased productivity. Previous OECD work has recommended integrating work-based learning more systemically into postsecondary education programmes through a regulatory framework in Israel (Musset, P., M. Kuczera and S. Field, 2014). Within Israel, there is an opportunity to develop more apprenticeship and other-work based training programmes, which are specifically targeted at Arab-Israelis. This would also require employer buy-in at the local level to ensure that these work-based learning opportunities are well connected to local job opportunities. The government could consider launching pilot programmes that would enhance partnerships between training institutions and employers.

Box 4.3 Recent apprenticeship initiatives within the United States

Apprenticeship 2000 Programme: The goal of the Apprenticeship 2000 programme is to offer high school students opportunities in technical career fields and employment after graduation. The programme, in return, offers sponsor employers a trained workforce. The employer contributes to a significant portion of the student's training. Recognising the need for trained craftsmen, Blum Inc., along with Daetwyler Corporation in 1995, established the Apprenticeship 2000 programme in an effort to train their own workforce. After graduation from the programme, students can earn upwards of USD 34 000 per year in their selected career fields.

The Apprenticeship 2000 programme is an 8 000 hour programme that spans four years of training. Upon graduation, students earn a degree in Manufacturing Technology, and a Journeymans Certificate awarded by the state of North Carolina. At graduation, each apprentice will have invested approximately 6400 hours inside one of the six sponsorship companies. The supplemental company instruction reinforces the student's classroom training by taking the classroom examples into real life situations. At Blum, company training is broken into three distinctive categories, each with their own sub categories. The three main categories are: Section One — Basic metal working/ bench work, Section Two — Machining (mill, lathe, CNC) and Section Three — Specialisation.

By training young people in basic machining, applications of engineering, and maintenance, Blum technicians become highly skilled to meet the needs of industry. Graduates of these technical career fields have the ability to design, machine, document and assemble changes virtually on demand. This makes each person and the company much more flexible to changes in trends, market conditions, and machine performance.

Box 4.3 **Recent apprenticeship initiatives within the United States** *(continued)*

Georgia Youth Apprenticeship Programme: In 1992, the Georgia General Assembly passed a law directing the Departments of Education, Labor, and Technical Adult Education to develop and implement youth apprenticeship programmes by 1996. Today, the programme operates successfully with more than 7,000 participants.

During their freshman and sophomore years of high school, students learn about the possibility of joining the apprenticeship programme as juniors and seniors. Students can then apply to participate in a structured programme of at least 2,000 hours of work-based training and 144 hours of related coursework. Apprentices complete not only their high school diploma, but also a postsecondary certificate or degree, and certification of industry-recognized competencies applicable to employment in a high-skill occupation. The fields vary widely from energy to information technology, manufacturing, and transportation and logistics. Mentorship is a key part of the programme, as are employer evaluations of the student's job performance and the building of professional portfolios. As of 2009, more than 7,000 students in Georgia were participating in a youth apprenticeship.

High schools are responsible for recruiting and counseling students, supporting career-focused learning, and assisting in identifying industry partners. Postsecondary schools participate in developing curriculum and dual credit arrangements. Businesses offer apprenticeship positions, provide each apprentice with a worksite supervisor, and ensure that apprentices gain experience and expertise in all the designated skill areas. The worksite supervisors must participate in mentor orientation and training so that they can guide students through all the skill areas and serve as coaches and role models. Parents must agree to and sign an educational training agreement and provide transportation to the student. Finally, apprentices must maintain high levels of attendance and satisfactory.

Source: OECD (2014), *Job Creation and Local Economic Development*, OECD Publishing, Paris. DOI: *http://dx.doi.org/10.1787/9789264215009-en*; Lerman, Robert (2012), Expanding Apprenticeship Opportunities in the United States, Brookings Institution, *www.brookings.edu/~/media/Research/Files/Papers/2014/06/19_hamilton_policies_addressing_poverty/expand_apprenticeships_united_states_lerman.pdf*

Recommendation: Introduce effective career guidance systems targeted to Arab Israelis, which ease school to work transitions and create transparent pathways which better connect high schools to the world of work

It would seem that where skills are fostered either through the higher or vocational education system, their translation into employment is limited by the absence of a comprehensive career guidance system. While the Employment Orientation Centres are engaged in customised guidance and job placements at the local level, a general system is lacking and needs to be integrated with both higher and vocational education tracks. A comprehensive career guidance system in Israel would need to be supported by good labour market intelligence. This intelligence can emerge not just out of formal data collection and analysis but also through informal information flows between participants in a 'skills ecosystem'. For Arab-Israelis, this could substitute for the informal networking offered by the army/national service systems, which creates significant inequalities in accessing quality job opportunities. This calls again for an integrated approach to skills supply and demand at the local level and the use of governance structures and networks that collate and share information across agencies and organisations.

Box 4.4 OECD experiences in providing career guidance

Northern Ireland: Each Further Education College also has a Careers Service that works with local employers to provide advice and guidance to students, each of whom has an Individual Learning Plan. Colleges are also heavily involved in career fairs and work placements with local firms. For example, Belfast Metropolitan College has recently opened a new E3 development in the west of the city. E3 (which stands for employment, economic development and enterprise) is a location for project-based learning, which seeks to bring students closer to employment or self-employment opportunities. Students work on a business project for an employer for a six week period while undertaking enterprise and entrepreneurship training.

Korea: To improve the labour market information available to job seekers, as well as the efficiency of public employment services, Korea established WorkNet, which is a the national online platform. This online portal serves as a one-stop shop for jobseekers, where employment offers certified by Job Centres are listed, and where vacancies are further customised to target various groups, such as youth, older workers, and women. The site also provides a voice-operated service for people with physical disabilities otherwise prevented from using the site. Other improvements to the services provided through WorkNet include a "Soft Matching" mechanism launched in 2010, which provides greater access to and an increased amount of labour market information. Since the second half of 2012, a "two-way service" has allowed clients of WorkNet to submit online applications to SMEs, who can send job offers by SMS or e-mail to qualified applicants.

Ontario, Canada: Career guidance is being redesigned to target younger students to ensure young people have good information to make labour market decisions and to ensure that postsecondary educational pathways are clearly articulated into either college or university. Ontario's colleges engage in a number of activities to ensure high school students are aware of their programme offerings. Efforts are made along with high school career counselling often in the second year of secondary education to create awareness of college offerings. A number of dual credit programmes are being offered that allow high school students to complete their studies while at the same time beginning a college programme. For example, the Mohawk College Bridge Programme allows students to simultaneously complete two credits towards their Ontario Secondary School diploma while gaining two elective credits towards their college programme as a part time college student at Mohawk.

Source: OECD (2014), *Employment and Skills Strategies in Canada*, OECD Reviews on Local Job Creation, OECD Publishing, Paris. DOI: http://dx.doi.org/10.1787/9789264209374-en;
OECD (2014), *Employment and Skills Strategies in Northern Ireland*, United Kingdom, OECD Reviews on Local Job Creation, OECD Publishing, Paris. DOI: http://dx.doi.org/10.1787/9789264208872-en;
OECD (2014), *Employment and Skills Strategies in Korea*, OECD Reviews on Local Job Creation, OECD Publishing, Paris. DOI: http://dx.doi.org/10.1787/9789264216563-en

Effective career guidance systems can help individuals reflect on their goals and ambitions while planning what education and skills are needed for a job. They help to better connect the education and training system to the world of work. Secondary schools in Israel need to work more closely with the public employment service and vocational education system to create clearer, simpler and more recognised pathways into vocational education and training, especially for Arab-Israelis and other disadvantaged groups.

There is also scope to better trace career pathways into employment-intensive domestic sectors that have high-growth potential. Transparent education pathways can play a vital role in better connecting the education and training system with the labour market. Good quality information can assist young people and adults in making informed choices about training programmes. This includes career guidance within high schools and as well occupational information about future job openings, their educational requirements, and earnings prospects.

Targeting policy to local employment sectors and investing in quality jobs

Recommendation: Place a stronger emphasis on the quality of jobs and the better utilisation of skills to stimulate overall productivity within the local labour market

A key pillar of job quality is improving the utilisation of skills of those already at work. This requires not only considering how skills are provided by the education and training system, but the extent to which employers develop and utilise skills. OECD research has shown that local public agencies can contribute to improving how skills are put to use by using a number of different policy instruments, such as incentives for employers to invest in new technology and the promotion of more effective forms of work organisation (Froy and Giguère, 2010). Investment in the supply of skills alone will not be sufficient to secure job creation and productivity in all local economies. The degree to which local employers are demanding and using skills also has to be taken into account. Where the demand for skills among employers is low, and people's skills are not fully utilised, this can undermine productivity. It can also reduce the quality of local jobs in terms of salaries, job security and the possibility for career progression.

Employment Orientation Centres have a mandate to focus on job placement therefore much of their focus is on creating labour market flexibility and ensuring 'work first'. This is attained through transportation to employment centres, child care, flexi-working hours, and the provision of local industrial/employment zones. All of these are supply-side activities. More attention will need to be directed to how these supply side interventions relates to demand locally. For example, the provision of industrial areas in Arab villages can easily end up being an exercise in land use zoning rather than economic development if it is undertaken without examining market demand signals. Similarly, transporting Arab women to entry level jobs distant from their place of residence may match the 'work first' ethos but it may not do very much in term of creating a positive labour market experience if the employment being offered is temporary, below minimum wage and without social benefits.

In Israel, there seems to be a lack of strategic focus on the better utilisation of skills as the public sector does not play a strong role in this important public policy area. While the national government is involved in a host of tangible and visible supply side initiatives to raise the overall level of skills, these are not complemented by approaches on the demand side to raise the overall quality of jobs. Local authorities in Israel are 'local' in jurisdictional responsibilities but myopic in economic perspective. Their approach to local economic development and job creation is grounded in property tax revenues. They play a very limited role in discussions of the quality of jobs and type of jobs to be attracted or fostered in the local economy. This is partly due to limited local fiscal autonomy and highly centralised funding frameworks.

Similarly, at the national level, the primary emphasis is on getting people into jobs. Limited attention is given to the length and sustainability of the job placement, prospects for mobility and career progression or overall pay. For a local area, such as the Yizreel sub district, this would seem paramount in order to progress beyond the low skill equilibrium trap that characterizes its economy with a number of poor quality jobs on offer. To prevent it from further disadvantage, more efforts are needed to promote quality employment opportunities that raise levels of income and lead to more mobility (social and employment) opportunities.

This involves a delicate balance between skill supply and demand side efforts. For government agencies and public authorities, the demand side is difficult to influence. The encouragement of a large anchor institution can act as the mediator in these instances, such as a hospital or a nursing home/retirement centre. It can generates demand for skills of all levels, boosts labour force participation across an range of groups in the labour force, meets rising demand for such a service in Arab society and also aligns with the growing trend of Arab workers to enter the medical and paramedical field. OECD research has identified the following tools to raise the overall quality of jobs:

Guidance, facilitation and training

- Support technology transfer: facilitating investment in new technology by employers, setting up partnerships for the sharing of innovation and new technologies.
- Provide technical assistance to improve working conditions and work organisation: this may mean the re-professionalisation of front-line positions in some sectors and a reduction in dependence on temporary staff, while in others it may mean better problem solving in the workplace. Providing staff with enough time to pass on skills and learning is also important.
- Encourage participation in training for both managers and workers: better trained managers are likely to create more productive working environments for their staff. At the same time, companies need to be encouraged to make training and other skills development opportunities available to their employees.

Influencing broader public policies

- Remove local disincentives to a focus on quality in the public sector: this may include changing incentive structures for local employment agencies so that they concentrate on the quality and not just the quantity of job-matches.
- Ensure that skills policies are embedded in economic development policies: local partnerships are needed between business and policy makers in the sphere of economic development, education and employment, in order to ensure that skills policies are understood in the context of broader economic development.

Box 4.5 **Practice labs for innovative work organisation, Flanders, Belgium**

In Limburg in Flanders, "Practice labs for innovative work organisation" have been set up to work with businesses on work organisation issues. The ACV union has played a key role in establishing and implementing the initiative.

The practice labs have been set up in the construction, logistics, healthcare, social economy, social service/care sector and agricultural sectors. Separate labs were established for each sector but in practice, labs can work with mixed groups, and can support both large and small firms. Eight workshops have taken place in 2013/14, each involving 6-8 companies. A consultant was hired to work on the workshops. They function as a learning network where companies share experience. Managers are encouraged to consider where they can effect change to make sure that workers have more involvement in the way that the firm operates.

Each lab covers seven themes, each of which is a different area where the manager can have an influence. One theme, for example, has been exploring new ways that firms can expand their market base to improve the quality of their organisation (in terms of efficiency, flexibility, quality, innovation, sustainability) while also improving job quality. Supervisors play the role of coach and act as a sounding board for participants who have questions, both within and outside of the lab sessions. Participants receive assignments to translate theory into practice when they return to the workplace. Unions report that the workshops have improved their relationships with local employers.

Source: OECD (2015), *Employment and Skills Strategies in Flanders, Belgium*, OECD Reviews on Local Job Creation, OECD Publishing, Paris.

Recommendation: Continue to stimulate entrepreneurship opportunities among the Arab-Israeli population to create more and better jobs

Entrepreneurship has a crucial role to play in modern societies due to its contribution to the generation of new ideas, innovation, job creation and economic growth. It has potential for creating jobs and reducing unemployment, not just in the population in general, but also among people who are vulnerable to social exclusion (OECD, 2014).

To successfully start up and operate a business, entrepreneurs need to use a wide range of skills. This skill-set includes skills that are required from employees in any workplace, but also those skills needed to respond to the additional demands of running a business (OECD/European Commission, 2013). While some of these skills may not be absolutely necessary for successfully operating a business, possessing them is likely to increase the quality of an entrepreneur's business and the chances that it will be sustainable and grow. It is therefore important to identify the skills needed by entrepreneurs and consider how they may be acquired and strengthened, and how this can be supported by public policy.

In Israel, there is a strong focus on providing entrepreneurship opportunities to the Arab-Israeli population. In Nazareth, a business incubator specifically targeted to the Arab population has been established and is providing critical training, networking, and mentoring opportunities to create new jobs in the community. These types of practices should be replicated in other areas of Israeli, where there is a higher proportion of Arab-Israeli residents.

For youth, providing adequate entrepreneurship training opportunities and access to financing is critical to stimulate job creation. OECD research on youth entrepreneurship has identified the importance of developing entrepreneurship skills; providing information, advice, coaching, and mentoring; providing financial support; and developing the entrepreneurship infrastructure as critical policy tools available to government policy makers to encourage entrepreneurial activities (OECD, 2013)

Box 4.6 Entrepreneurship programmes for youth

Youth Entrepreneurship Programme, California, United States: The Youth Entrepreneurship Programme presents the perfect opportunity for innovative young adults in Orange County, Los Angeles County and the Inland Empire Region to learn, network, and compete in a business plan competition for scholarships. Through a variety of events, seminars, activities, and working sessions, participants, ages 18-27 years of age, will understand how to develop their creative entrepreneurial side and re-invent their notions of "tomorrow".

For students and young entrepreneurs who have a business or business idea and are looking to take the first steps towards success, the Youth Entrepreneurship Programme holds an annual business plan competition where high school and college students compete for scholarships. For anyone who has ever had a business, a great idea or simply wants to immerse themselves in the entrepreneurial community, the Youth Entrepreneurship Programme holds a variety of events meant to connect entrepreneurs and aspiring entrepreneurs. For young entrepreneurs who have already started a small business and are looking to grow it, the Youth Entrepreneurship Programme offers YEP 2.0. This is an intensive series of seminars and workshops that focus on taking your business to the next level.

.garage Hamburg (Germany): The programme provides work space for up to 45 young entrepreneurs at a time. Entrepreneurs apply with a business plan and are eligible to receive up to EUR 5000 in start-up capital. Projects are supported in creative and professional programmes such as music, literature, art, film, design, broadcasting company/television, showing arts, architecture, press, advertisement and software/games.

Applicants first visit a start-up assessment centre where they discuss their business plan. Start-up capital of EUR 500–3000 is available at a low interest rate and loans are awarded based on the business plan and the individual's dependability and potential.A key component of the garage is that young entrepreneurs are supported by professional experts. They provide advice, deliver weekly seminars on finance, distribution and time management; training sessions on special topics; and help build networks. A coaching service is also available at a cost of EUR 10/hour for up to 12 weeks of on-the-job coaching in areas such as: advertisement and distribution, growth financing, accounting, organisation and time management.

Source: Youth Entrepreneurship Programme, www.my-yep.org/about/; OECD (2013) Policy Brief on Youth Entrepreneurship, OECD Publishing, www.oecd.org/cfe/leed/Youth%20entrepreneurship%20policy%20brief%20EN_FINAL.pdf

Being inclusive

Recommendation: Use government procurement more strategically by establishing conditions within contracts to support inclusive growth and increase labour force participation among Arab-Israelis

The use of public procurement as a means of local economic development and to promote job quality should be more fully explored in Israel, especially as it pertains to increasing labour force participation of Arab-Israelis. It is important to remember that the public sector can play an important role in helping to shape skills demand and utilisation locally, not only as a policy maker but also as a purchaser of services (Froy et al, 2012).

Governments should ensure that the public sector at the local level has the necessary capacity to influence its local supply chain. This includes being able to require training, apprenticeship and employment opportunities for local people when putting construction, regeneration and other development activities out to tender. Public procurement can be used as a strategic tool to meet wider objectives and can ensure that more public expenditure is focused on having a positive impact. For example, national tenders can specify other conditions such as apprenticeship provisions that have the long-term effect of building the local skills base.

Box 4.7 Using public procurement for social inclusion, city of Most, Czech Republic

The city of Most in the Czech Republic applied the condition that as part of four public contracts for the construction of flats in the Chanov quarter (a socially deprived locality) and one public contract for cleaning, 10% of all those hired had to be long-term unemployed. The cleaning services contract was awarded to a firm that hired one long-term unemployed person. Other long-term unemployed were also hired on short-term contracts. Candidates were put forward by local non-profit organisations and were mainly people with low levels of education, skills and work experience who, according to senior staff, were able and willing to learn. Five out of seven persons stayed in their job after completion of the contract and two were offered a permanent contract. The newly hired workers performed preparatory technical work, finishing and ancillary works.

Applying the 10% condition in tendering contracts did not burden bidders or make the contract more expensive for the city. The firms have been considering not only fulfilling the mandatory 10% quota but hiring other long-term jobless. The city of Most has incorporated the procurement terms into the Integrated Development City Plan and is considering how it can be applied to other contracts. The Agency for Social Inclusion has included the example of Most in a manual for municipalities to encourage them to take similar approaches.

Source: OECD (2014), *Employment and Skills Strategies in the Czech Republic*, OECD Reviews on Local Job Creation, OECD Publishing, Paris. DOI: http://dx.doi.org/10.1787/9789264208957-en

References

Ben-David D (2012) (ed.), *State of the Nation Report, Society, Economy and Policy in Israel 2011-12*, Taub Center for Social Policy Studies, Jerusalem.

Brookings Institution (2012), *Global Metro Monitor 2012*, Metropolitan Policy Program, Brookings Institution, Washington DC.

Field S and Kuczera M (2012), *A Skills Beyond School Commentary on Israel*, OECD Reviews of Vocational Education and Training, Paris.

Lerman, Robert (2012), Expanding Apprenticeship Opportunities in the United States, Brookings Institution, *www.brookings.edu/~/media/Research/Files/Papers/2014/06/19_hamilton_policies_addressing_poverty/expand_apprenticeships_united_states_lerman.pdf*

MOITAL (2012), *Progress Report on the Implementation of the OECD Recommendations: Labour Market and Social Policies*, Israel, Ministry of Industry, Trade and Labor, Jerusalem.

Musset, P., M. Kuczera and S. Field (2014), *A Skills beyond School Review of Israel*, OECD Reviews of Vocational Education and Training, OECD Publishing. DOI: *http://dx.doi.org/10.1787/9789264210769-en*

OECD (2015, forthcoming), *Employment and Skills Strategies in Flanders, Belgium*, OECD Reviews on Local Job Creation, OECD Publishing, Paris. DOI: *http://dx.doi.org/10.1787/9789264228740-en*

OECD (2014a), *Job Creation and Local Economic Development*, OECD Publishing. DOI: *http://dx.doi.org/10.1787/9789264215009-en*

OECD (2014b), *Employment and Skills Strategies in Canada*, OECD Reviews on Local Job Creation, OECD Publishing. DOI: *http://dx.doi.org/10.1787/9789264209374-en*

OECD (2014c), *Employment and Skills Strategies in the Czech Republic*, OECD Reviews on Local Job Creation, OECD Publishing. DOI: *http://dx.doi.org/10.1787/9789264208957-en*

OECD (2014d), *Employment and Skills Strategies in Northern Ireland*, United Kingdom, OECD Reviews on Local Job Creation, OECD Publishing. DOI: *http://dx.doi.org/10.1787/9789264208872-en*

OECD (2014e), *Employment and Skills Strategies in Korea*, OECD Reviews on Local Job Creation, OECD Publishing. DOI: *http://dx.doi.org/10.1787/9789264216563-en*

OECD (2014f), *Employment and Skills Strategies in the United States*, OECD Reviews on Local Job Creation, OECD Publishing. DOI: *http://dx.doi.org/10.1787/9789264209398-en*

OECD (2013a), Policy Brief on Youth Entrepreneurship, OECD Publishing, *www.oecd.org/cfe/leed/Youth%20entrepreneurship%20policy%20brief%20EN_FINAL.pdf*

OECD (2013b), *Review of Recent Developments and Progress in Labour Market and Social Policy in Israel: Slow Progress Towards a More Inclusive Society*, OECD Publishing, Paris. DOI: *http://dx.doi.org/10.1787/9789264200401-en*

OECD/The European Commission (2013), *The Missing Entrepreneurs: Policies for Inclusive Entrepreneurship in Europe*, OECD Publishing, Paris. DOI: *http://dx.doi.org/10.1787/9789264188167-en*

OECD (2010), *OECD Reviews of Labour Market and Social Policies: Israel*, OECD Publishing, Paris. DOI: *http://dx.doi.org/10.1787/9789264079267-en*

Persky J., Felsenstein D and Carlson V (2004), *Does 'Trickle Down' Work? Economic Development Strategies and Job Chains in Local Labor Markets*, W.E .Upjohn Institute of Employment Research Kalamazoo, MI

Yashiv, E. and N. Kasir (2011), Patterns of Labor Force Participation Among Israeli Arabs, *Israel Economic Review*, 9 (1),. 53-101.

Yashiv, E. and N. Kasir (2013a), *Arab Women in the Israeli Labor Market: Characteristics and Policy Proposals*, Israel Economic Review, 10 (2),.1-41.

Yashiv, E. and N. Kasir (2013b), *The Labor Market for Arab Israelis: Characteristics and Policy Choices*, Department of Public Policy, Tel Aviv University, *www.tau.ac.il/~yashiv/IsraeliArabs_policy_paper.pdf*

Annex A. Communities included in the study area

Sub District[1]	Name	Identification code	Population 2012 (Th)[2]
Sub District 23 Yizreel- Afula	Ramat Yishai	0122	7.2
	Yokne'am Illit	0240	20.3
	Dachi	0475	0.6
	Achksal	0478	13.0
	Daboriya	0489	9.4
	Mukibala	0635	3.3
	Migdal Ha'Emek	0874	24.4
	Shibli-Um El Ganem	0913	5.4
	Bosmat Tivon	0944	7.1
	Zarzir	0975	6.9
	Afula	7700	41.7
	Bet Shean	9200	17.2
Sub District 25 Yizreel-Nazereth	Buena-Nujidat	0482	8.5
	Turan	0498	12.7
	Yafia	0499	17.7
	Kefar Kana	0509	20.0
	Ilut	0511	7.2
	Mashhad	0520	7.4
	Ein Mahel	0532	11.8
	Romana	0539	1.0
	Kabia	0978	4.6
	Nazeret Illit	1061	40.8
	Nazareth	7300	74.0
Sub District 30 Haifa	Dalit El Carmel, Ussafiya	0494	16.0
	Rechasim	0922	9.7
	Tirat HaCarmel	2100	18.6
	Kiryat Tivon	2300	17.3
	Nesher	2500	23.2
	Haifa	4000	272.2
	Kiryat Atta	6800	52.7
	Kiryat Motzkin	8200	38.9
	Kiryat Bialik	9500	38.2
	Kiryat Yam	9600	38.3

1. The Central Bureau of Statistics (CBS) combines sub districts 23 and 25 into one subdistrict (Yizreel 23). The Ministry of Interior separates them into separate administrative units. This study follows the former.
2. CBS (2013), *Statistical Abstract of Israel 2012*, Table 2.24.

Source: CBS (2013), *Statistical Abstract of Israel 2012*.

Annex B. Gross regional product estimates

The regional allocation method uses the following sources of data:

- Residential Stock: this is created from baseline (stock of the number of built square meters used for residential dwellings 2008) and the yearly change before and after the base year. Source of data for the base year is the CBS data on property tax collection by square meters. Yearly change comes from CBS data on completed residential dwellings in sq m.
- Capital Stock: this is generated from a baseline stock (commercial and industrial built floor space 2008) and the yearly change before and after the base year. Source of data for the base year is CBS data on property tax collection by square meters. Source of the yearly change is CBS data on completed commercial and industrial buildings, floor space, sq m). Monetary value of capital (plant and machinery) is distributed by the square meter stock for each district.
- Compensation: Data on average monthly wage of employed persons comes from CBS income surveys and National Insurance Institute data by district. Number of employed persons in each district is from CBS work force surveys.
- GDP Data: National GDP and National Income data source is CBS Statistical Abstract of Israel. The data includes total GDP and total Net National Income.

In addition we use share of the Net National Income which comes from the three major sources of income:

- Compensation of employed persons residents.
- Domestic operating surplus from owner occupied dwellings.
- Domestic operating surplus excluding owner occupied dwellings (surplus from capital gains).

The Allocation Method is based on estimating Gross Regional Income for the 6 districts of Israel as follows:

- The share of Net National Income for each of the three sources is distributed by the share in the relevant stock of each district.
- For each region the three major sources of Net Income are summed to create the share of each district region in the National Net Income.
- The share of each region in the National Net Income is multiplied by national GDP to create the Gross Regional Income.

Summarizing:

$$GRP_{it} = \left(\left(\frac{W_{it}}{\sum_{i=1}^{6} W_{it}} \cdot SW_t\right) + \left(\frac{R_{it}}{\sum_{i=1}^{6} R_{it}} \cdot SR_t\right) + \left(\frac{K_{it}}{\sum_{i=1}^{6} K_{it}} \cdot SK_t\right)\right) \cdot GDP_t$$

Variables:

W_{it} – Compensation for employed persons in district in year.

R_{it} – Residential stock in square meters in district in year.

K_{it} – Capital stock of plant and machinery in district in year.

SW_t – Share of compensation of employed persons in the Net National Income in year.

SR_t – Share of domestic operating surplus from owner occupied dwellings in the Net National Income in year.

SK_t – Share of capital gains in the Net National Income in year.

Annex C. Comparing labour market outcomes in the case study areas

Figure C.1 **Male wages, 2000-20111**

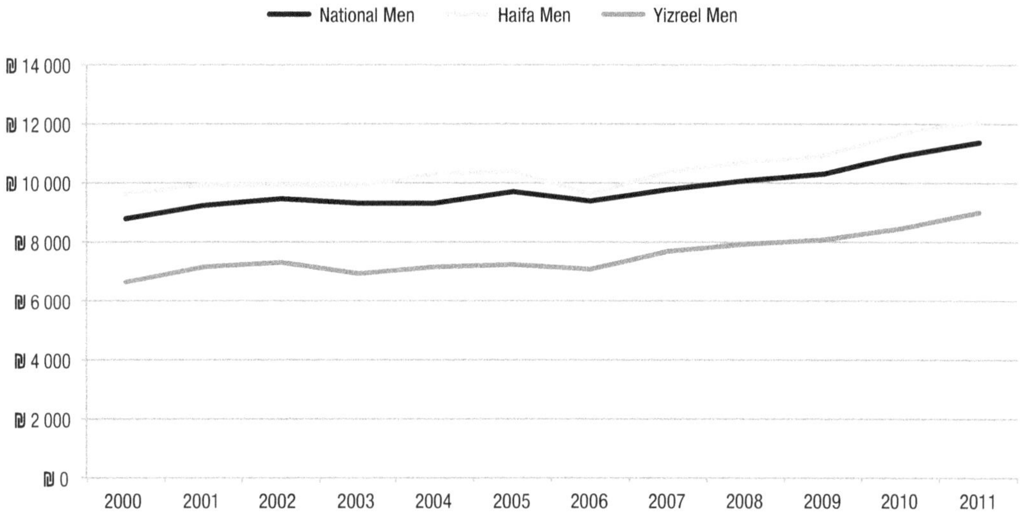

Source: Central Bureau of Statistics (CBS), 2012.

Figure C.2 **Female wages, 2000-2011**

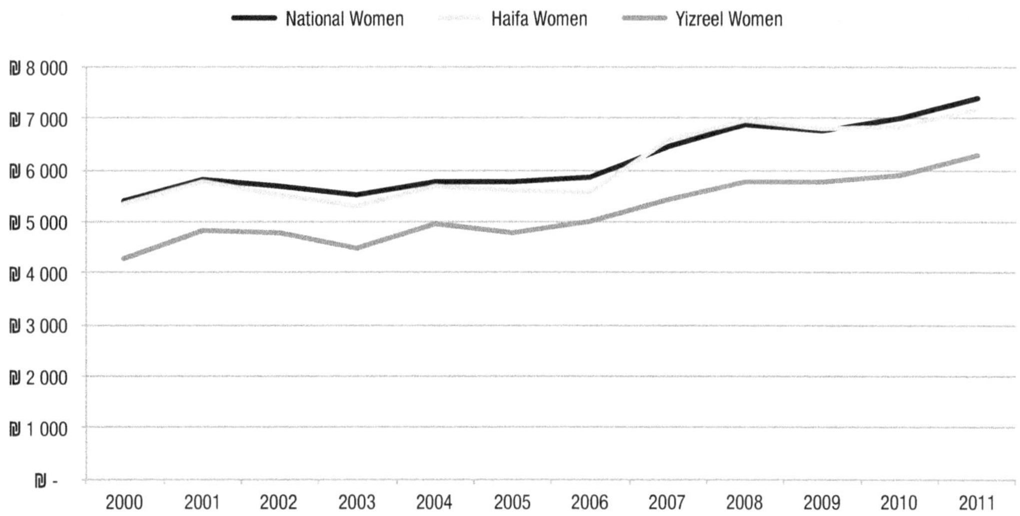

Source: Central Bureau of Statistics (CBS), 2012.

Figure C.3 **Female labour market participation by sub-district, 2000-2011**

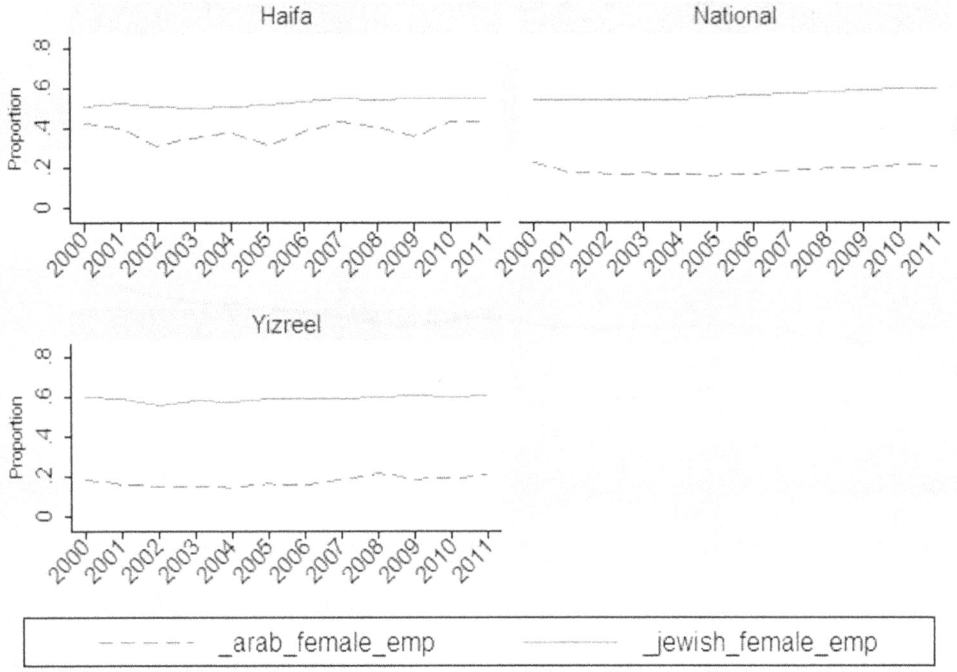

Source: Central Bureau of Statistics (CBS), 2012.

Figure C.4 **Male labour force participation by sub-district, 2000-2011**

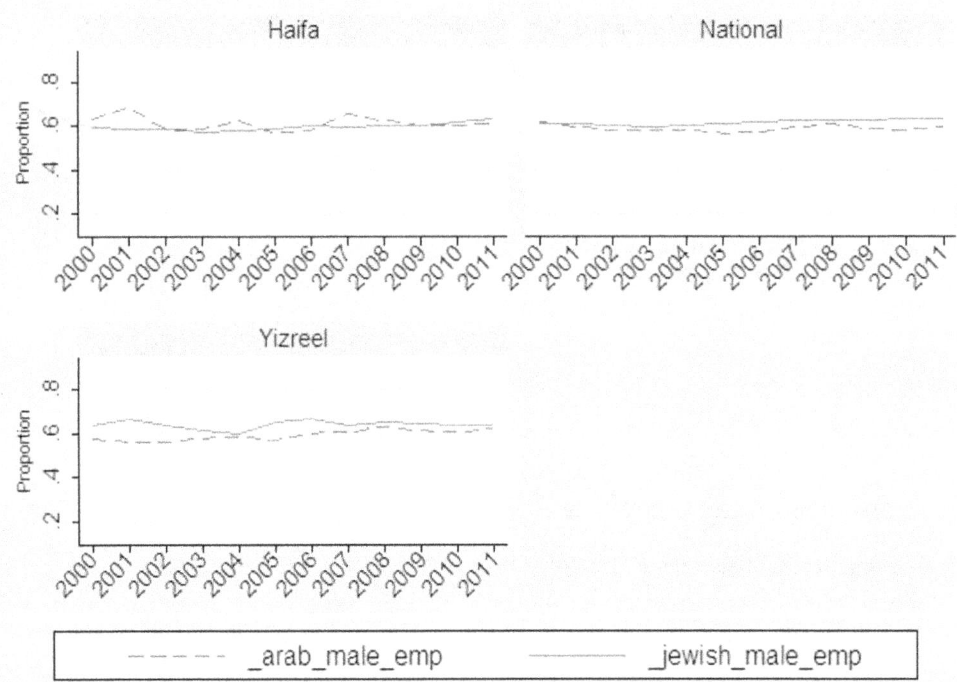

Source: Central Bureau of Statistics (CBS), 2012.

Figure C.5 **Youth labour force participation by sub-district, 2000-2010**

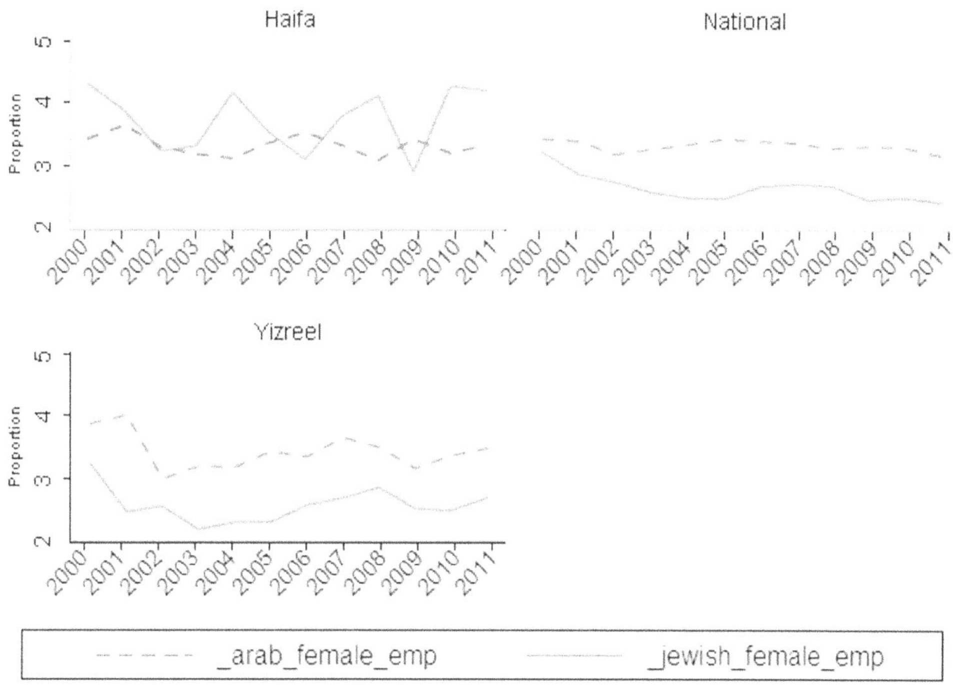

Source: Central Bureau of Statistics (CBS), 2012.

Figure C.6 **Labour force participation of older works (over 50 years), 2000-2010**

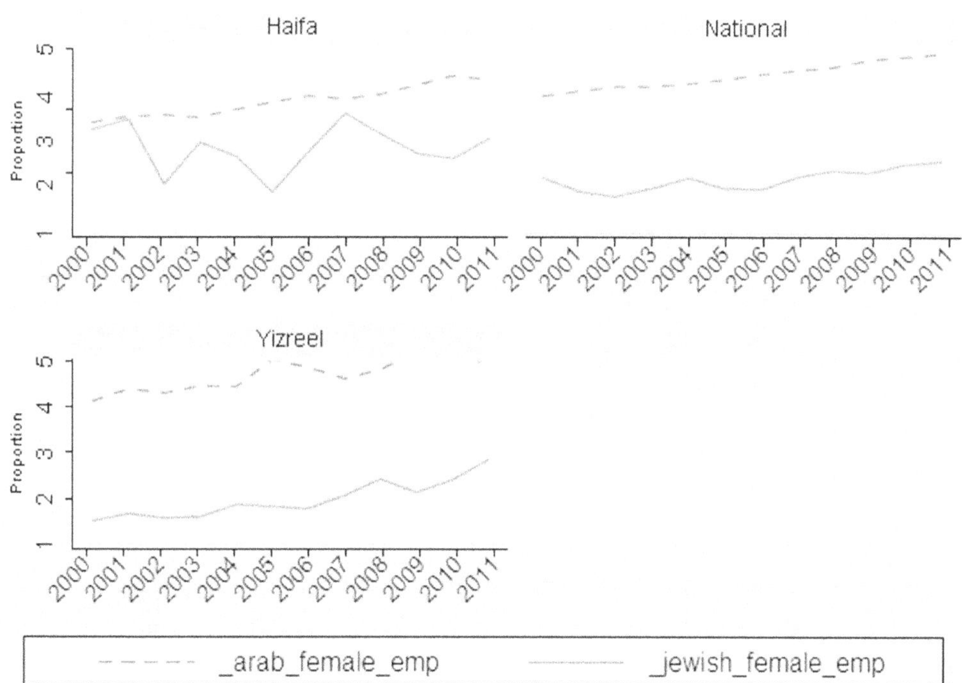

Source: Central Bureau of Statistics (CBS), 2012.

Figure C.7 **Female unemployment by sub-district, 2000-2011**

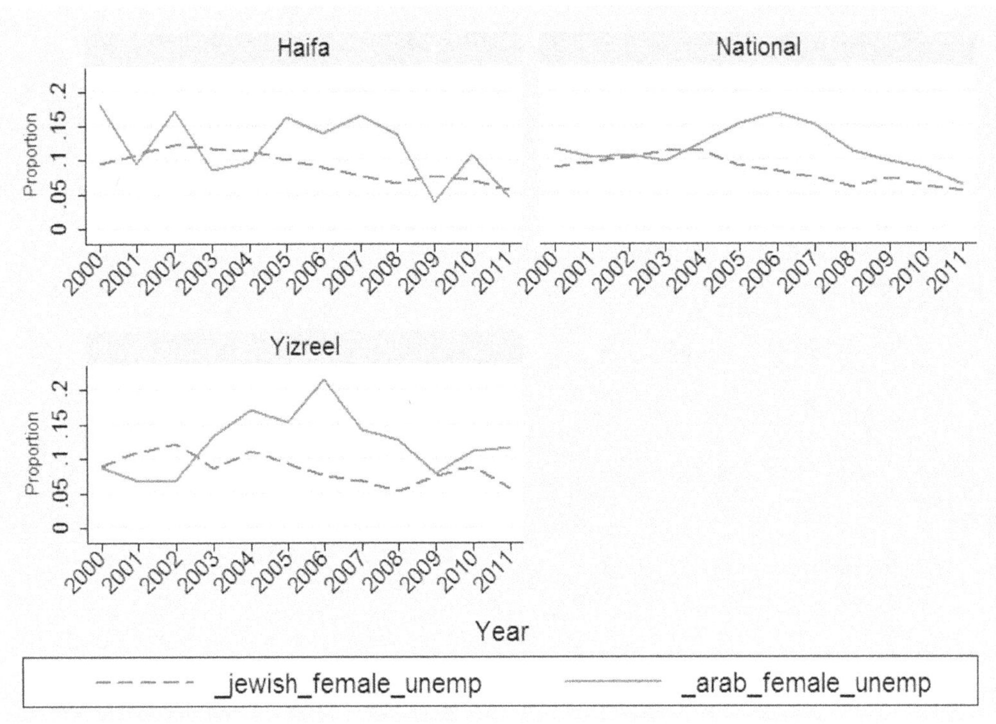

Source: Central Bureau of Statistics (CBS), 2012.

Figure C.8 **Male unemployment by sub-district, 2000-2010**

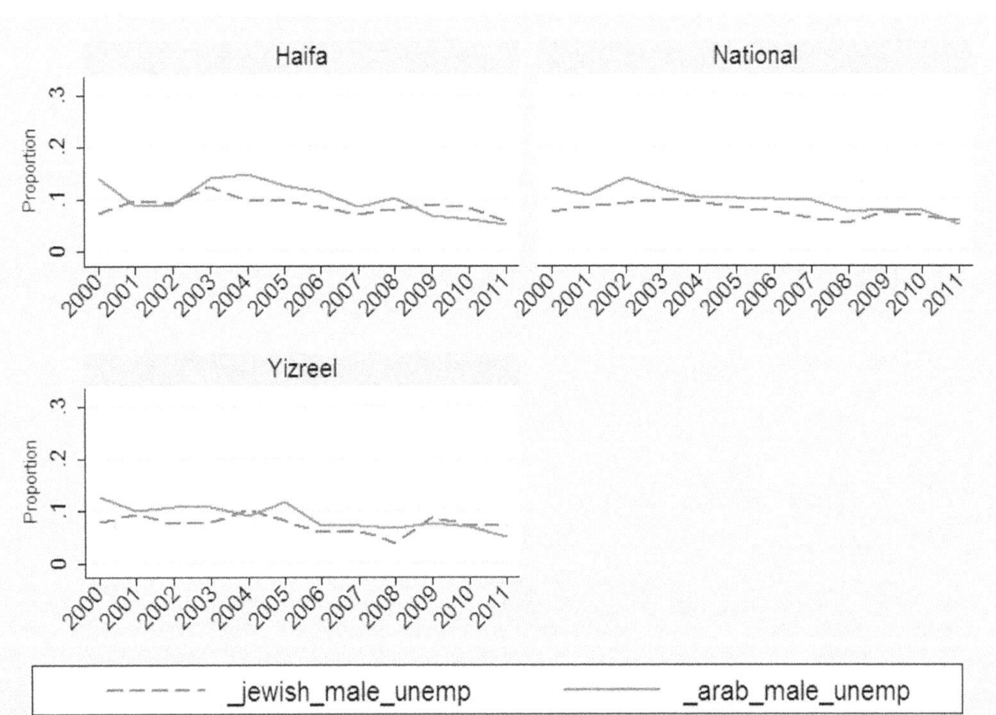

Source: Central Bureau of Statistics (CBS), 2012.

Figure C.9 **Youth unemployment (15-24) by sub-district, 2000-2010**

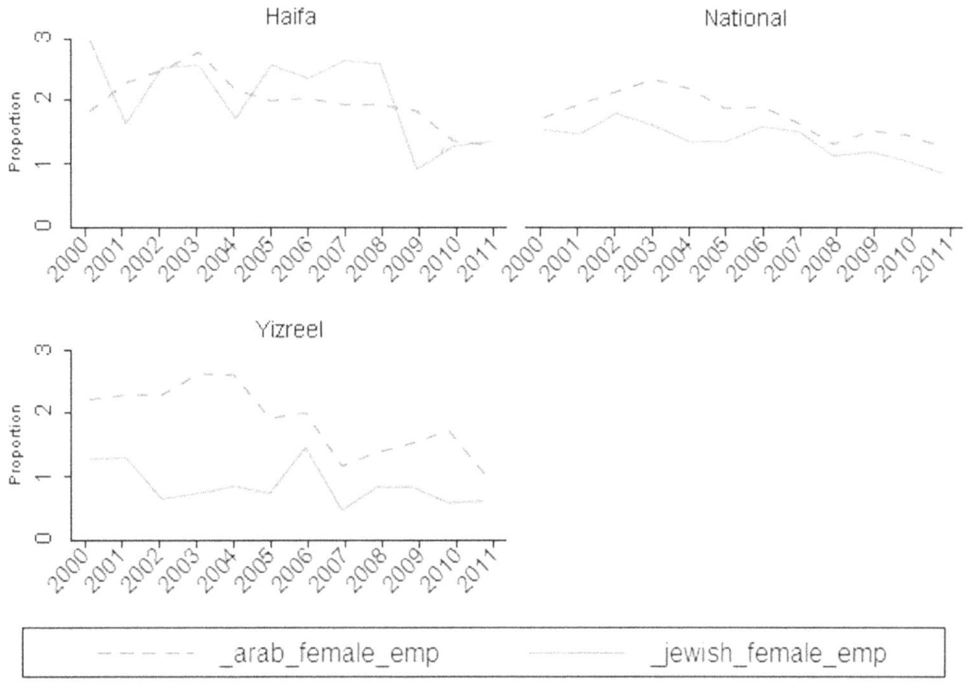

Haifa
National
Yizreel
Proportion
0
1
2
3
2000
2001
2002
2003
2004
2005
2006
2007
2008
2009
2010
2011
_arab_female_emp
_jewish_female_emp

Source: Central Bureau of Statistics (CBS), 2012.

Figure C.10 **Unemployment among older workers (over 50 years), 2000-2010**

Haifa
National
Yizreel
Proportion
0
0.05
0.1
1.5
2
2000
2001
2002
2003
2004
2005
2006
2007
2008
2009
2010
2011
_arab_female_emp
_jewish_female_emp

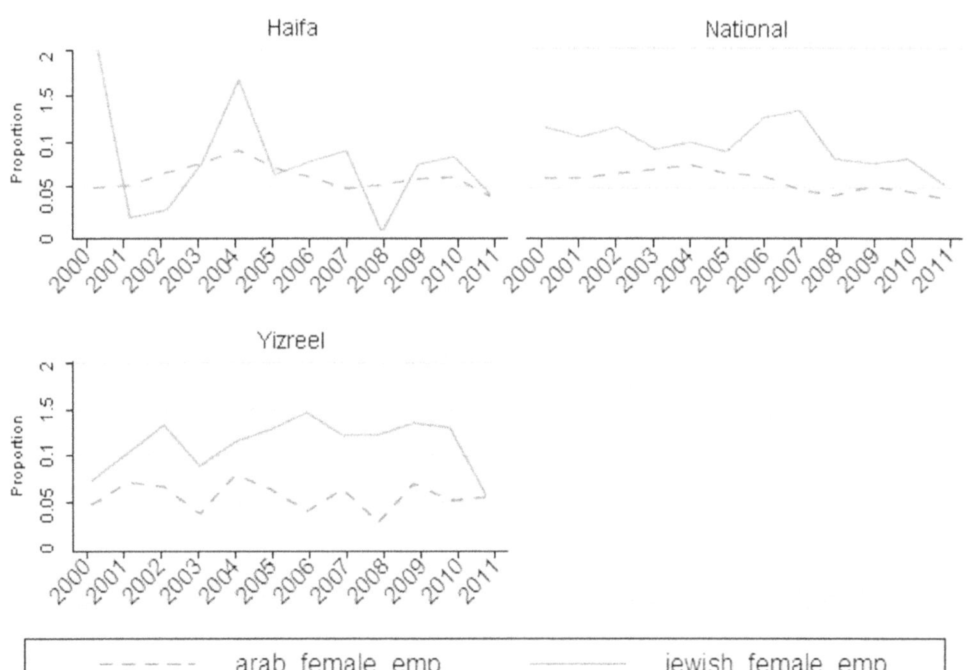

Source: Central Bureau of Statistics (CBS), 2012.

Figure C.11 **Job search: proportion actively looking for work- Jewish and Arab female labour force, 2000-2011**

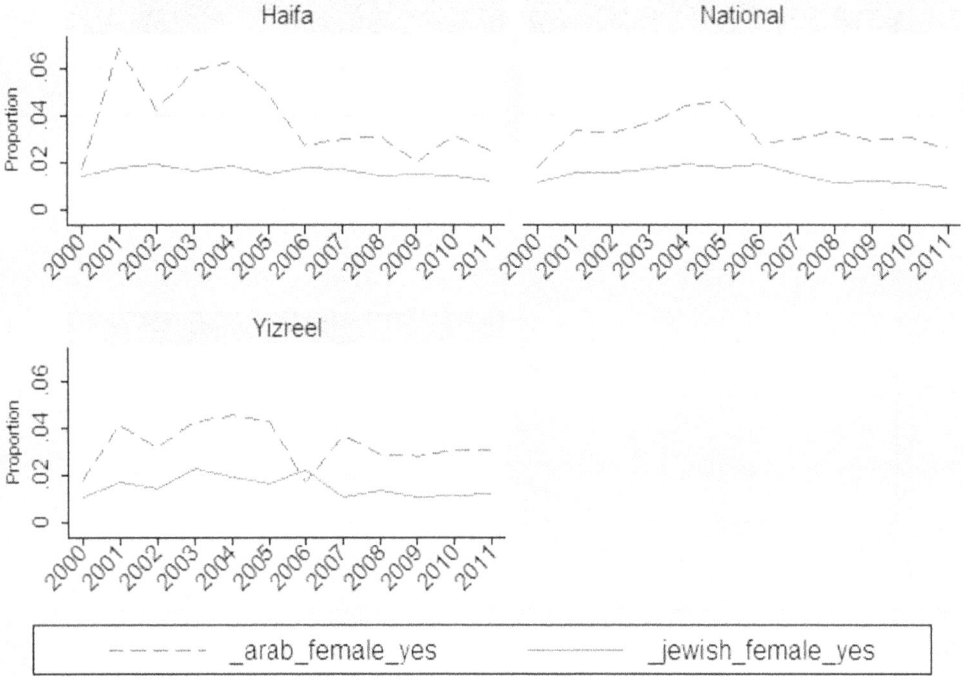

Source: Central Bureau of Statistics (CBS), 2012.

Figure C.12 **Job search: proportion actively looking for work - Jewish and Arab male labour force, 2000-2011**

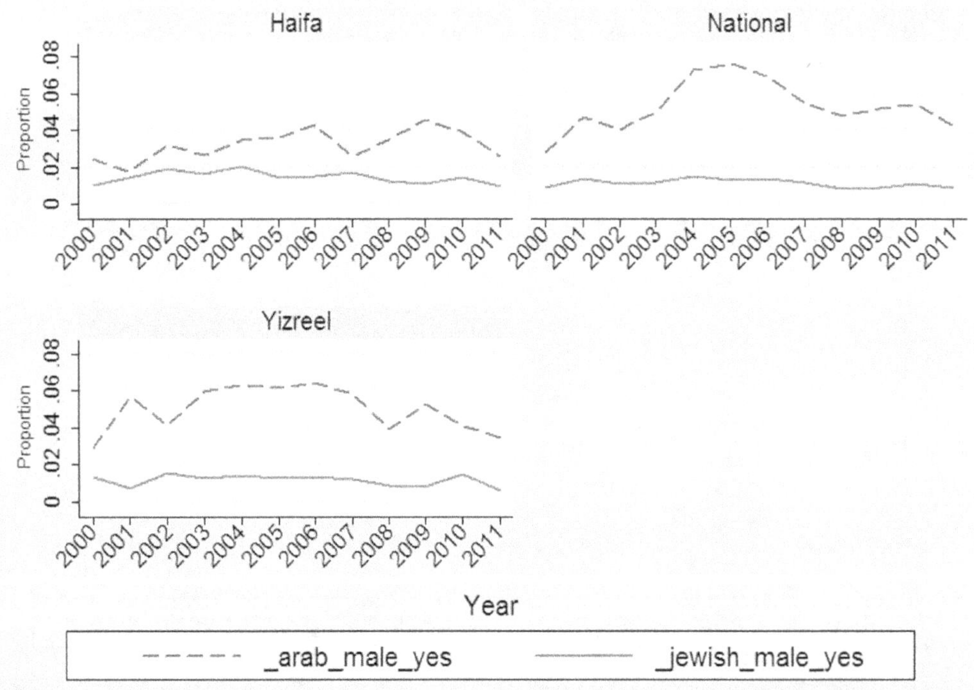

Source: Central Bureau of Statistics (CBS), 2012.

Figure C.13 **Arab female labour force, 1-8 yrs and 16+ yrs education, 2000-2011**

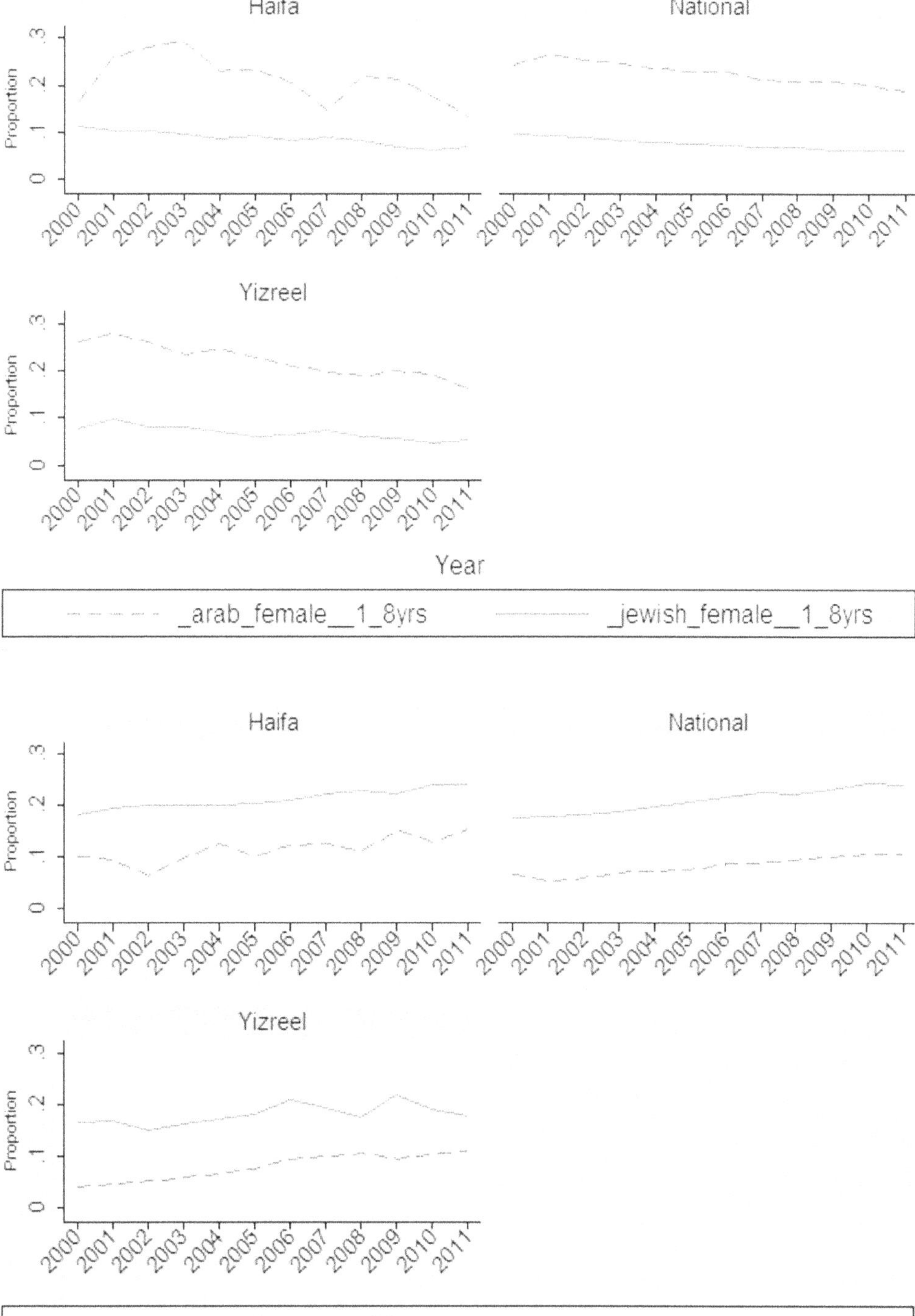

Source: Central Bureau of Statistics (CBS), 2012.

Figure C.14 **Arab male labour force, 1-8 yrs and 16+ yrs education, 2000-2011**

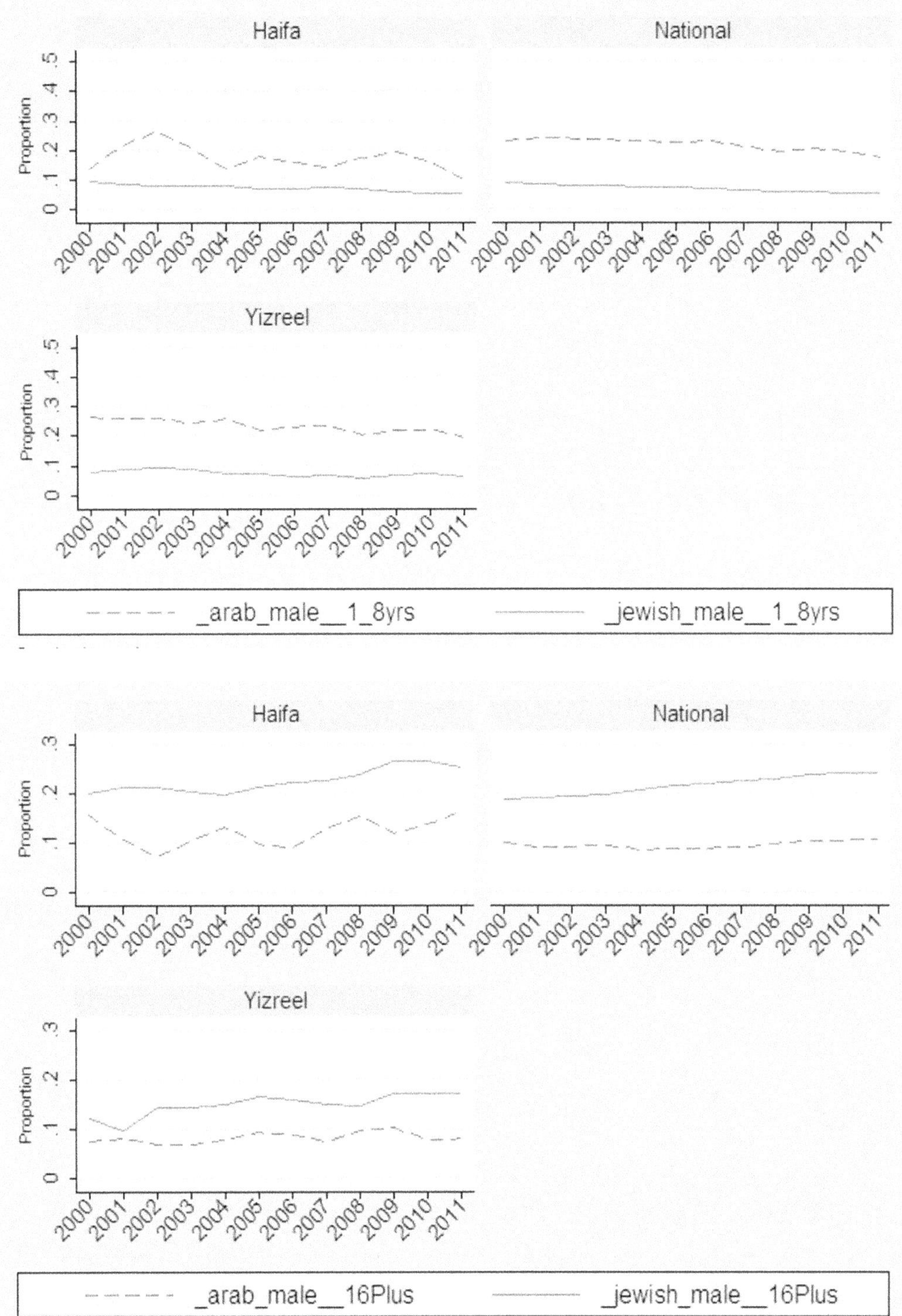

Source: Central Bureau of Statistics (CBS), 2012.

Annex D. Regression results

Table D.1 **Panel regressions for wages and labour participation rate (t stats* in parentheses)**

	(A) Wages		(B) Labour participation rate				
	(1) Male	(2) Female	(3) Male	(4) Female	(5) Jew	(6) Arab	(7) All
Method	Panel	Panel	Panel	Panel	Panel	Panel	Panel
Labour participation rate	-1.0604	0.6975					
	(-2.72)	(2.00)					
Age	-1.4250		-0.49367		-0.9654		-0.5478
	(-1.58)		(-1.77)		(-5.17)		(-2.14)
Education	0.4513	0.0861	0.3659	0.6824	0.3838	1.1464	0.6769
	(1.03)	(1.65)	(2.57)	(3.51)	(3.25)	(5.42)	(4.91)
Length job search	-0.0920	-0.0704					
	(-2.09)	(-1.51)					
Non-commuters			0.0414	0.0322	0.0297	0.0545	0.0263
			(2.05)	(2.12)	(2.04)	(2.22)	(2.15)
Constant	0.0485	0.05603	0.0002	0.0059	0.0060	-0.0060	0.0022
	(6.72)	(6.70)	(0.11)	(1.75)	(2.79)	(-1.07)	(1.02)
N	51	51	63	63	63	63	63
R-squared	0.26984	0.1969	0.1725	0.2445	0.4519	0.4210	0.3731
DW stat	1.55	1.69	2.27	2.46	2.25	2.25	2.34
Region	Fixed Effect	Fixed Effect	Fixed Effect	Fixed Effect	Fixed Effect	Fixed Effect	Fixed Effect
Haifa	-0.00502	-0.0064	0.00179	0.0019	0.0015	-0.0015	0.0023
National	-0.00264	-0.0003	0.00061	0.0014	0.0002	-0.0005	0.0008
Yizreel	0.00766	0.0068	-0.00181	-0.0033	-0.0017	0.0021	-0.0031

* The t-statistic is a ratio of the departure of an estimated parameter from its notional value and its standard error.

Source: Central Bureau of Statistics (CBS), 2012.

ORGANISATION FOR ECONOMIC CO-OPERATION AND DEVELOPMENT

The OECD is a unique forum where governments work together to address the economic, social and environmental challenges of globalisation. The OECD is also at the forefront of efforts to understand and to help governments respond to new developments and concerns, such as corporate governance, the information economy and the challenges of an ageing population. The Organisation provides a setting where governments can compare policy experiences, seek answers to common problems, identify good practice and work to co-ordinate domestic and international policies.

The OECD member countries are: Australia, Austria, Belgium, Canada, Chile, the Czech Republic, Denmark, Estonia, Finland, France, Germany, Greece, Hungary, Iceland, Ireland, Israel, Italy, Japan, Korea, Luxembourg, Mexico, the Netherlands, New Zealand, Norway, Poland, Portugal, the Slovak Republic, Slovenia, Spain, Sweden, Switzerland, Turkey, the United Kingdom and the United States. The European Union takes part in the work of the OECD.

OECD Publishing disseminates widely the results of the Organisation's statistics gathering and research on economic, social and environmental issues, as well as the conventions, guidelines and standards agreed by its members.

LOCAL ECONOMIC AND EMPLOYMENT DEVELOPMENT (LEED)

The OECD Programme on Local Economic and Employment Development (LEED) has advised governments and communities since 1982 on how to respond to economic change and tackle complex problems in a fast-changing world. Its mission is to contribute to the creation of more and better quality jobs through more effective policy implementation, innovative practices, stronger capacities and integrated strategies at the local level. LEED draws on a comparative analysis of experience from the five continents in fostering economic growth, employment and inclusion. For more information on the LEED Programme, please visit *www.oecd.org/cfe/leed*.

OECD PUBLISHING, 2, rue André-Pascal, 75775 PARIS CEDEX 16
(84 2015 08 1) ISBN 978-92-64-23295-2 – 2015

www.ingramcontent.com/pod-product-compliance
Lightning Source LLC
LaVergne TN
LVHW081419110826
845149LV00010B/1797

* 9 7 8 9 2 6 4 2 3 2 9 5 2 *